THE BOOK OF
MATCHA

THE BOOK OF MATCHA

Superfood Recipes for Green Tea Powder

Louise Cheadle
and Nick Kilby of

teapigs.

STERLING EPICURE

New York

STERLING EPICURE
New York

An Imprint of Sterling Publishing Co., Inc.
1166 Avenue of the Americas
New York, NY 10036

Sterling Epicure is a trademark of Sterling Publishing Co., Inc. The distinctive Sterling logo is a registered trademark of Sterling Publishing Co., Inc.

This Sterling Epicure edition published in 2017 by Sterling Publishing Co., Inc.

© 2016 by Louise Cheadle and Nick Kilby

ISBN: 978-1-4549-2218-6

Distributed in Canada by Sterling Publishing c/o Canadian Manda Group, 664 Annette Street Toronto, Ontario, M6S 2CD, Canada

For information about custom editions, special sales, and premium and corporate purchases, please contact Sterling Special Sales at 800-805-5489 or specialsales@ sterlingpublishing.com

Manufactured in China

10 9 8 7 6 5 4 3 2 1

www.sterlingpublishing.com

First published in 2016 in the United Kingdom by Jacqui Small LLP

Illustrations by Emma Cobb

Food photography by David Munns

Contents

INTRODUCTION

Welcome to our book all about matcha. We are **Louise Cheadle** and **Nick Kilby**, the founders of teapigs, and we are big fans of this superhero among teas.

"What is matcha, and why is it so good for you?" you may ask. Matcha is a superpower tea made only from green tea leaves and containing natural flavonoids (catechins). The best matcha comes from Japan and is shade-grown before being ground to a very fine powder.

Drinking matcha is like drinking ten cups of regular green tea for its nutrient value—that's why we call it superpower green tea. We think a daily dose of all-natural matcha will give you buckets of sprightliness!

One of the reasons matcha is so good for you is that the tea bushes grow under lots of shade, which boosts their chlorophyll content (that's the bright green stuff). The leaves are picked by hand and the stems and veins removed, leaving only the best, juiciest part of the leaves. The leaves are then ground to make a super-fine, vibrant green, nutrient-rich powder.

Another reason matcha is so good for you is the way it's drunk. When you drink regular green tea, you throw away the leaves afterwards, which is a bit like boiling spinach, throwing away the spinach and just drinking the water—you will get some of the nutrients, but you're throwing away the best bit. With matcha, you ingest the whole tea leaf so you're consuming every little bit of that lovely green-tea good stuff.

Matcha is believed to give you a slow release of energy that lasts throughout the day while keeping you calm, alert, and focused at the same time. That's why Japanese students drink it when they're cramming for their exams, and it's also why Buddhist monks drink matcha to keep them calm and focused during hours of meditation.

Matcha is a very versatile ingredient: Not only can it be drunk hot, but it can be mixed with juices, milk, cold water or even made into a cocktail. Because matcha is a powder, it also can be used for cooking—anything from breakfast granola and snacks to stir-fries and desserts—just look at the recipe section from page 50 for a wealth of ideas on how to include matcha in your daily diet.

This book is our introduction to matcha. We have included how matcha came about, its importance in the Japanese tea ceremony, how it's produced and consumed today, the reasons that people love it, and its numerous health benefits. We also have included a huge selection of varied recipes so you can enjoy matcha at any meal—including sweet and savory dishes and a wide range of drinks.

We introduced matcha to our range of teas in 2008. At that time, matcha wasn't readily available in the UK, but we absolutely loved it, and we knew other people would too (once they understood what it was!). Having sourced the very finest bright-green matcha we could find, we put it in a quirky little box with our matcha man design (Mr. Nishio). We took the box to Selfridges in London, who were very happy to put it on their shelves.

Matcha became an instant hit with teapigs' customers, and we worked really hard to educate more and more people about the power of our matcha, its amazing versatility, and the way it makes you feel super. We now have matcha in big tins, little tins, individual (on-the-go) sachets, and blended into ready-made drinks. We run a matcha challenge every year, with great feedback from our customers on how energized they feel.

We enjoy matcha daily not only because it tastes great, but because it's all-natural and powerful stuff, packed with nutrients. We also love the fascinating history behind this bright-green tea and the unique way in which it's produced. We hope that our book will inspire you to enjoy matcha every day too.

Louise   Nick

The
History of
Matcha

Matcha's origins

Although you may have discovered matcha—the super-concentrated 100 percent green tea powder—only recently, it is nothing new. Matcha has been drunk in Japan since the twelfth century, and before that in China. Although the Japanese are considered the masters of matcha, key elements of matcha production originated in China.

In China, drinking green tea was commonplace in the eighth century, and the tradition of steaming and drying green tea into bricks was widespread. Then the Chinese Zen (Chan) monks got involved. They broke off chunks from the brick and ground it into a very fine powder using a pestle and mortar, before whisking the powder with hot water in a large bowl to make their green tea. The whisking of the ground green tea leaves became a key part of the Zen Buddhist daily ritual.

Matcha came to Japan when Myoan Eisai, a Japanese monk, discovered ground green tea leaves while traveling in China in the late 1180s to study Zen Buddhist meditation. In love with China, Zen Buddhism, and ground green tea leaves, he returned to Japan in 1191 with a few tea plant seeds. He then began a very successful one-monk campaign to popularize Zen Buddhism within Japan and promote the consumption of matcha, which he believed was vital for meditation.

Myoan Eisai (1141–1215), Zen Master

Eisai was the founder of the Rinzai sect of Zen Buddhism and was known as a great reformer. Not only did he bring tea plant seeds from China, he also wrote widely of the health benefits of tea and matcha. His book Kissa Yojoki, *which means "Drinking Tea for Health," was published in 1211 and was the first book about tea published in Japan. The first line reads: "Tea is the ultimate mental and medical remedy and has the ability to make one's life more full and complete."*

Eisai believed the Chinese lived a long and healthy life due to their consumption of tea and its medicinal properties, and he encouraged the Japanese to take on this tea drinking habit.

MATCHA IS "THE ELIXIR OF THE IMMORTALS"
EISAI

The Chinese moved on to other teas, including pu-erh, oolong, and black tea (which they call red tea). Meanwhile, in Japan, the popularity of green tea developed further, with matcha soon becoming an intrinsic part of Japanese life.

Left Zen Master, Myoan Eisai, who brought matcha from China to Japan.

Above Zen monks of the Soto School meditate at the Seiryu-ji Temple in Hikone City, Japan.

The Japanese Tea Masters

Tea masters spend years perfecting the spiritual and ritual practices of the tea ceremony. In the fifteenth and sixteenth centuries there were a number of important grand tea masters:

Ikkyu Sojun (1394–1481)
A Japanese Zen Buddhist priest, poet, and tea master, he was one of the great influencers. Credited with an edgy and eccentric approach to Buddhism, he was respected for his great tea practice.

Murato Shuko (1422–1502)
A disciple of Ikkyu Sojun (see above), Murato Shuko is considered the father of the early Japanese tea ceremony, which is also known as the Way of Tea (page 14).

Takeno Joo (1502–1555)
The teacher of Sen No Rikyu (see below), Taken Joo was an advocate of Zen simplicity and humility.

Sen no Rikyu (1522–1591)
Sen no Rikyu is credited with developing the details of the Cha-no-yu, or Japanese tea ceremony (page 14), that are still key today. Rikyu was the tea master for Oda Nobunaga, a Japanese warrior chieftain, and introduced the concept of the slow-paced tea ceremony, making it part of every tough feudal negotiation.

MATCHA GROWS IN POPULARITY

Zen monasteries in Japan embraced the matcha movement as the monks found that the long periods of meditation were easier with matcha inside. The L-theanine (whether they knew it) kept them calm and alert for long periods of time. (See "The Health Benefits," page 32.)

Enjoying matcha became part of the cultural tradition and the artistic life of Japan. Those who enjoyed poetry, music, and high society activities also enjoyed the luxurious (and expensive) matcha. As the Samurai, aristocrats, and intellectuals began to understand and appreciate matcha, it grew in popularity over the centuries, in particular toward the end of the sixteenth century. At this time, having your very own tea master (page 11) to make your matcha at home became the norm among the Japanese elite.

GROWING TEA IN JAPAN OVER THE CENTURIES

Ancient records suggest that the very first batch of tea seeds were planted in Japan in around 805 by two monks, Saicho and Kukai. Following the method they had seen on a trip to China, they pressed the leaves into bricks, and then put scrapings from the bricks into hot water. Emperor Saga fell in love with tea and encouraged the propagation of tea in Japan, but it wasn't until Eisai (page 10) promoted matcha in Japan and brought tea to his friend, the priest Myoe, in Kyoto, that production really took off.

In the 1190s, Myoe took matcha plants to many locations including Uji, southeast of Kyoto, where tea cultivation flourished. This region has a climate suited to tea production, with limited frost and a mild but constant wind, and is renowned today for the excellent quality of teas produced there. (See page 29.)

Tea producers began to develop and enhance their production techniques in order to optimize the growing, shading, and grinding of the very best matcha. It's thought that the shading of the bushes (known as Tana, page 26) was introduced in the sixteenth century.

In 1738, Soen Nagatani established the Uji green tea processing method. This is a standard production method still used throughout Japan today. He steamed the tea leaves to stop the fermentation process—a method now called Sencha (page 24). The Uji method/Sencha gives a fresh, green taste to the leaves.

This development was key to tea production in Japan, making Japanese green tea unique and different from the pan-fired or roasted green teas of China. The matcha process includes a gentle

steam after the leaves have been picked to retain freshness.

Matcha production has been refined over the years, and very different qualities of matcha are now available (page 28). The number of matcha producers has increased, and the standards can vary dramatically between them (page 52).

MATCHA IN THE TWENTY-FIRST CENTURY

Matcha was one of Japan's best-kept secrets, but it's increasingly consumed around the world. Matcha is a key component of the Japanese tea ceremony (page 14), where ceremonial-grade matcha is used. Matcha is also widely consumed as a beverage in Japan, and there are several different grades of matcha for drinking (page 52).

In addition, the demand for "ingredient"-grade matcha has increased in recent years as matcha began to be used in both sweet and savory foods. In the last ten years, matcha has found its way into some very mainstream products—from ice cream and Kit Kats to bread and Oreo cookies. See Matcha Today, page 42.

Left Japanese women in traditional clothes inside a tea house, Tonosawa, Japan, c.1880.

Above Workers on a tea plantation in Uji, Japan, c.1890.

MATCHA HISTORY AT A GLANCE

700s
Green tea made from dried tea bricks drunk widely in China.

960–1129
Chinese Song Dynasty. Steaming and grinding of tea to make a fine powder became popular.

1103
Monastic "Chanyuan Qinggi" written, describing the etiquette for tea ceremonies in China.

1191
Myoan Eisai, a Japanese monk and founder of Zen Buddhism, brought tea seeds from China, and cultivation and production of matcha started in Japan.

1336–1573
Japanese Muromachi period. Matcha became popular with the Samurai warrior class.

1522
Sen No Rikyu born. He became a great tea master and formalized the rituals of the Japanese tea ceremony or Cha-no-yu.

1500s–2000
Matcha and the tea ceremony firmly established in Japanese cultural life.

21ST CENTURY
Matcha growing in popularity around the world, and is found in everything from cupcakes and croissants to salads and milkshakes.

THE TEA CEREMONY

The Japanese tea ceremony, also called the Way of Tea, focuses on the preparation and serving of matcha in the presence of guests. Although this highly stylized ceremony varies depending on factors such as the season and those participating, it's known worldwide as a very respectful and peaceful experience.

In Japanese, the tea ceremony is known as Cha-no-yu (also as Chado or Sado), which roughly translates as "hot water for tea."

That sounds so simple, doesn't it? Thankfully, from a tea lover's perspective, the tea ceremony is anything but simple.

The Four Main Principles of Cha-no-yu

The guiding principles of Cha-no-yu as expressed by Sen No Rikyu (tea master) are:

 Complete harmony between guests, hosts, and surroundings. This starts from the moment you step into the tea garden.

 Profound respect for all, regardless of rank or status. Respect is shown by kneeling and bowing throughout the ceremony.

 To cleanse yourself and be of pure heart and mind. The tea house is supposed to be a refreshing space, the equivalent of a yoga studio!

 Inner peace that you can discover only by obtaining the first three principles of Wa, Kei, and Sei.

In addition to these principles, the essence of Cha-no-yu is summed up in ichi-go ichi-e, which literally means "one time, one meeting." Participants should be conscious that each tea gathering is a unique occasion, so sincerity is key.

Over the centuries the Japanese have perfected the art of tea drinking and preparation. The ritual ceremony is a magical, slow process where the tea is central to a series of precise movements. Enjoyment happens in two parts: enjoyment of the slow, calm, and relaxing steps to make the tea; and enjoyment of the tea itself.

The tea ceremony was developed fully by the sixteenth century, with professional tea masters such as Sen No Rikyu (page 11) developing the intricate details that make up the rituals of the ceremony. Every factor is important, from the type of tea, to the ceramics, fashion, painting, flowers, architecture, and even the gardens around the tea house. These rituals, surroundings, and equipment remain today in Cha-no-yu.

Monks and members of high society traditionally led the tea ceremony as tea masters, but over time women became increasingly involved in the ceremony, and today women far outnumber men in the practice of Cha-no-yu.

Above Tea master preparing matcha: taking water with a bamboo ladle (hishaku) from an iron pot (known as a kama or chanoyugama).

WHAT THE TEA CEREMONY INVOLVES

The Japanese tea ceremony centers on the preparation and serving of matcha in the presence of guests, and a full-length ceremony can last about four hours. Each act is designed to focus the senses on the task at hand, and distractions are kept to a minimum.

Each ceremony is unique and will differ depending on those participating, the time of day, the season, and the room where it's taking place. That said, the basic procedure for the preparation of the tea always follows certain time-honored steps (opposite) and uses key ceremonial utensils (page 18).

Traditionally the tea ceremony takes place in a room adorned with simple artworks and is accessed by crawling through a low door, thus the participants are required to bow immediately and express humility. The tea master leading the ceremony will have spent years perfecting these ceremonial rituals.

Traditional tatami mats are placed on the floor, and the room is surrounded by Shoji screens, which are window frames filled with paper, shielding the view from distractions, while allowing light in. Ideally a small garden will surround a tea house.

Interior of a traditional Japanese countryside tea house. Tea houses vary in style and size, but simplicity is key.

1 The host greets the guest with a bow at the entrance gate. The entrance may be low so the bow is forced.

2 The guest washes his or her hands in a stone wash-basin and removes his or her shoes before entering the tea house, which is common practice in all Japanese homes and traditional buildings.

THE CEREMONY

3 The tea urn, scoop, and bowl are wiped down in a symbolic gesture of purification of the utensils.

4 Using the scoop, the host transfers the matcha into the bowl and adds hot water from a kettle using a bamboo ladle. The mixture is then mixed with a bamboo whisk.

5 The guest is offered the freshly made matcha tea. The guest should thank the host graciously with a slight bow of the head.

6 The bowl should be placed in the left hand and guided to the lips with the right. If there is more than one guest, the first guest wipes the area from which he or she has just drunk and passes the bowl to the next guest, who will drink from the same place as the first guest; this gesture symbolizes the bonding of all those taking part.

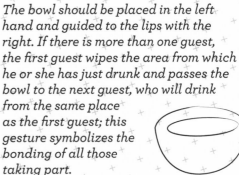

7 At a full-length ceremony a small meal will be served, however in shorter versions a sweet treat will be offered at the start.

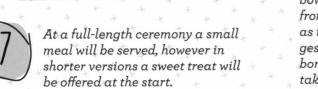

TEA CEREMONY TOOLS

Many utensils are used during the tea ceremony. Collectively they are called "dogu." The top three must-haves are the chasen (bamboo whisk), chashaku (tea scoop), and chawan (tea bowl).

CHASEN *(bamboo whisk): This is the vital element for making matcha. The whisk is carved from a single piece of bamboo and comes with a varying number of prongs. Outside the beautiful world of the tea ceremony we recommend using a speedy milk frother. However, inside the tea house, nothing but this bamboo whisk will do.*

CHASHAKU *(tea scoop): Usually carved from bamboo, the Chashaku tea scoop stylishly transfers the matcha from its container to the bowl. It takes a little bit of practice as we are far too accustomed to using a spoon!*

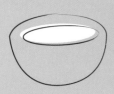

CHAWAN *(tea bowl): In the same way that we have a favorite cup or mug, the tea master will have a favorite bowl. Some may be ancient and works of great art, hand thrown or heavily decorated. Others may be smaller, plainer, and just a little cheaper. In summer, shallower bowls are used so the matcha chills more quickly. In winter, deep, high-sided bowls are used to keep the tea warm longer.*

The list of equipment for the tea ceremony is never-ending. Here are some other utensils you may want to use:

Chabako *(storage box for utensils): A solid box containing a set of utensils. A traveling tea master will bring his or her own kit.*

Chaki *(pot): The essential pot used to hold the matcha tea during the ceremony.*

Dora *(copper gong): The host gives this a big bang when he or she is ready for the guests.*

Hachi *(bowl for food/sweets): The special bowl used to present the "sweet treat" that accompanies the matcha.*

Kama/Chanoyugama *(iron pot): A traditional iron pot used to heat the water for the tea ceremony.*

Kuromoji *(chopsticks): These wooden chopsticks are used to eat the sweet treats. No fingers!*

Neriko *(incense): A lovely blended incense, burned during the ceremony.*

Tenmoku *(tea bowl): A unique tea bowl with narrow feet.*

THE DOS AND DON'TS OF THE TEA CEREMONY

Tourists are often keen to experience a traditional Japanese tea ceremony, and for a fee many places offer this service with an expert or "host" to guide them through the process (page 48). If experiencing the ceremony there are a number of points to remember.

1. First remove your shoes.

2. If you are game, a kimono will look the part and be respected; if not, "sensible" Western clothes are acceptable.

3. Enter the room on your knees. Traditionally there is a low door so you have no option but to shuffle in on your knees.

4. Use only closed fists to balance yourself as you shuffle forward, avoiding the middle of the tatami mats.

5. Know your place! If you find yourself at a tea ceremony, you need to know if you are the guest of honor (Shokyaku) or the second in line (Jikyaki). If you are neither of these, you are the Kyaku (a regular guest, don't feel bad!). The Shokyaku will be the first to have the matcha and will pass the bowl to the left, turning and wiping the bowl as it goes down the line.

6. The Shokyaku thanks the host. The other guests should sit politely and observe the beauty of the room.

SEASONAL CEREMONIES

Not all ceremonies are the same. These are the main seasonal ceremonies.

*In **November**, a ceremony celebrates the breaking of the seal on a new jar of tea (Kuchikiri-no-chaji). This is the first time the tea leaves harvested in the spring will be drunk. The start of the winter season is a great cause for celebration!*

*During the **winter season**, there are a dawn tea ceremony (Akatsuki-no-chaji) and a dusk ceremony (Yuuzari-no-chaji)—these are magical, cold, candlelit ceremonies in which you can enjoy sipping tea while watching the sun rise or set.*

*Held in **January**, the first ceremony of the year is the Hatsugama, commonly known as the first boiling of the kettle. This is the fancy ceremony, where all the best utensils and sweet treats come out.*

*The end of the tea supply happens in **October** with the Nagori-no-Chaji ceremony. This is a somber event, in which the guests display sad faces because of the empty tea jar.*

The Production of Matcha

All about tea

Matcha—like all tea—comes from the leaves of the tea plant, *Camellia sinensis*. This subtropical evergreen plant is related to the camellia, a decorative plant grown in gardens. There are two main varieties: *Camellia sinensis sinensis*, which is traditionally found in China; and *Camellia sinensis assamica*, which is traditionally found in Assam, India.

There are numerous types of tea, which vary widely depending on where they grow and how they are processed. For example, you will find only the best white tea growing in the Fujian region in China. The brisk, bright, black tea produced in Rwanda is unique to the mountain region of East Africa. The special fermentation process used in Taiwan generates the most unique oolong tea.

We think it's pretty incredible that one plant can produce so many unique flavors and tastes. The taste variation starts with where the plant grows—the geographical location, the soil, the altitude, and the weather patterns. The defining character is given to the tea by the way the leaves are treated after plucking (picking). This production process changes the final flavor of the tea dramatically.

A good tea is a well-made tea—one that has been looked after and finely crafted at every stage. Weather patterns can't be controlled, but the production stage can be managed very closely. Tea estates, generally, have to choose between making large volumes of "ok" tea or a smaller amount of something top-quality. If they choose the latter, they will pluck only the best leaves (the freshest shoots from the top of the bush) and process them very delicately, ensuring that they don't damage the leaf.

Japan is very much the home of genuine, world-class, gold-star matcha, so we will focus mainly on the Japanese tea industry.

Left Rows of fresh green tea bushes growing at a plantation in the Makinohara chabatake tea fields of Shizuoka Prefecture, Japan.

Right Gyokuro tea, a speciality green tea growing under shade in Japan.

Japanese green teas

The Japanese have taken tea making to a higher level with efficient mechanization, which puts them in a different league from other producers. Only a handful of countries do not pluck exclusively by hand, but the Japanese have managed to maintain the quality and artisanal approach of tea production despite using machines.

The range of teas produced in Japan is very wide but can be classified into broad categories. Here are our top six Japanese green teas, if you like, but the list is neverending.

1. MATCHA (THE BIG ONE!)

The secret to making matcha from regular green tea leaves is the delicate, complicated, slow production process as shown on pages 26–7. The taste of matcha is unique, and its umami flavor (page 45) can be compared to no other tea produced around the world. Its look is also very different, and although frequently confused with an instant powder, matcha is purely whole leaves ground down to make a super-fine powder.

2. SENCHA

Sencha is the most common grade of green tea and makes up about 70 percent of Japan's total tea production. As explained on page 12, the steaming process was introduced in Uji by Soen Nagatani, and it's the steaming that makes Japanese tea pretty special. The length of time that the tea is steamed for determines its taste: a 20-second blast gives a lighter-colored cup and a stronger aroma; whereas a longer steam (up to 160 seconds), which breaks up the leaves more, produces a darker-colored tea with a stronger flavor.

3. GENMAICHA

Genmaicha is made from a sencha green tea base (above) with toasted and puffed rice added to it. Historically, this tea blend came about as a way of making an expensive commodity (tea) go further. Made for centuries by the poor of Japan trying to save their tea supplies by adding rice, genmaicha

is now one of the most established drinks in Japan. Becoming increasingly popular around the world, this is a teapigs' favorite—we call it "popcorn tea" as it has hints of popcorn.

4. KUKICHA

Kukicha, also known as Bocha and "twig tea," is a mixture of bright-green sencha leaves (opposite), or sometimes gyokuro (right), with yellow leaf stems. Usually, we wouldn't expect good-quality tea made from the stems rather than the buds and leaves of the tea bush, but kukicha is a light, non-astringent, and tasty green tea. In addition, the stems don't contain as much caffeine as the leaves, so it's a naturally lower-caffeine drink.

5. HOJICHA

Hojicha is usually made from bancha tea leaves that have roasted in a porcelain pot over a charcoal fire at a high heat for a few minutes. This distinctive Japanese tea uses the final teas of the harvesting season, and the roasting helps to standardize the flavors. The leaves have a dark brown appearance—not the most appealing to look at, but very interesting to taste. The resulting tea is woody and nutty and has a distinctive brown rather than green color.

KNOW THE LINGO

Hachiju-hachiya—*88 nights from the start of spring.*
Tana—*shading over a rack system.*
Jikagise—*less sophisticated shading.*
Aracha—*unrefined tea prior to sorting.*
Tencha—*the base sorted tea prior to grinding.*
Matcha—*superpower green tea—the end result.*

6. GYOKURO

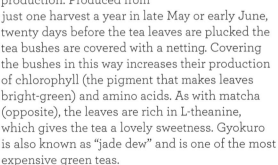

Gyokuro Tamahomare (its full name) is one of Japan's most precious teas, revered for its purity and richness of taste. Mainly grown around Kyoto, Japan's ancient capital, gyokuro makes up less than one percent of Japan's tea production. Produced from just one harvest a year in late May or early June, twenty days before the tea leaves are plucked the tea bushes are covered with a netting. Covering the bushes in this way increases their production of chlorophyll (the pigment that makes leaves bright-green) and amino acids. As with matcha (opposite), the leaves are rich in L-theanine, which gives the tea a lovely sweetness. Gyokuro is also known as "jade dew" and is one of the most expensive green teas.

Far left Grading the quality of tencha.

MATCHA PRODUCTION

The secret to making matcha, not just ground green tea leaves, is the complicated and delicate growing and production process it undergoes.

Over the winter, the tea bushes are dormant. As spring breaks at the end of March to early April, the tea buds begin to shoot. The fields of tea bushes at this stage are almost completely shaded. There are two different ways to shade the leaves—Tana and Jikagise.

Jikagise

Jikagise is used by small-scale growers. A large cloth goes directly over the tea bushes to shade them. This has a similar effect to the Tana method but offers less control.

Tana

Tana is used on the large, commercial, top-grade estates and is an elaborate cage that covers the whole field. The cage goes around the edge of the field and over the top of the tea bushes. Netting is spread over the cage with a gap between the roof and the tea bushes to allow growing space. This netting lets in just 10 percent of the light, yet allows rainfall and moisture to reach the tea bushes.

The **shading process** stresses the tea bush. If it could speak, it would be shouting: "More light, more light!" The tea bush can't photosynthesize, which creates more L-theanine (an amino acid) and prevents tannins from developing (the tannins give tea its harsh taste). L-theanine also provides the calm energy boost that we look for in matcha and gives a sweet umami taste to the tea (page 45).

The **harvesting** of the tea leaves starts from the 88th day after the start of spring, which is called "Hachiju-hachiya" in the traditional Japanese calendar. On a modern calendar this usually falls on May 1.

The **plucked leaves** go to the factory to be refined first into what is known as "aracha" and then into "tencha." The leaves are promptly steamed at a very high temperature to stop the fermentation or oxidization process—which also preserves the dazzling green color. The steaming is very short—just 20 seconds.

Then the leaves are dried slowly to lower the moisture content. At this stage, the leaves are called "aracha."

The **aracha** (meaning "rough tea" in Japanese) is refined further—the stalks, veins, and any imperfections are removed. This is done by sieving the leaves, sorting them, and using a machine called a color separator, which pulls out only the perfect bright green leaves for selection.

We now have **tencha**. The tencha is graded, and the graded leaves are ground in a stone mill to make the extremely fine powder we know as matcha.

The **stone mill** consists of two granite stones. The stones are engraved with a crisscross pattern, which forces the leaves from the inside of the rotating stones to the outside. The tencha leaves are fed into the gap at the top of the stone mill that joins the stones, which is known as the "fukumi." The tencha is sandwiched between the granite stones as they rotate against each other and grind the leaves into tiny particles. The end result is a grain of matcha measuring just 5–10 microns across—smaller than a grain of talcum powder!

The making of the matcha stone mill is an ancient Japanese art, and the grooves in the granite are carved by hand. The miniscule grooves are deeper at the edge of the stone than they are in the middle, which can be seen only with a magnifying glass. Maintaining these traditional granite stones is quite an art, and lifting them is another challenge!

The **grinding process** happens in a highly controlled environment. The temperature is cool, consistent, and humidity-free. The entirely mechanized process takes place in the dark to keep the leaves bright-green and fresh. The grinding process is very time-consuming. To make just one little tin of top-grade matcha takes a whole hour.

The final **matcha** is graded again by an expert tea taster to ensure quality. The ground leaves then go to the packing room, where, in darkened conditions, the top-grade matcha is vacuum-packed into tins. These tins keep out the light and retain all the freshness of the matcha.

Know your matcha

What is the difference between a green tea powder and matcha? How can you know that you have bought the best matcha and not a poor imitation? There are a number of points to look for when buying matcha, including where it's from, its color and feel, and its cost.

What are the key differences between a green tea powder, which is also marketed in Japan, and a genuine matcha powder?

MATCHA POWDER

Grown in the shade

Bright-green leaf

Steamed

Umami taste (page 45)

Vibrant color in cup

GREEN TEA POWDER

Not grown in the shade

Brown/yellow leaf

Pan-fired

Bitter taste

Murky color in cup

WHAT'S IN A NAME?

There are lots of different types of matcha—ingredient versus premium, ceremonial versus cooking, culinary versus classic. All these descriptions can be very confusing.

Looking at it very simply, some matcha is better for drinking than cooking and some is better suited to cooking. If you're baking matcha croissants or muffins, then ingredient-grade matcha will work well. If you're re-enacting the tea ceremony with fancy guests, then you will need the finest, ceremonial-grade matcha. Unfortunately, the words ceremonial and premium are used freely and don't fall under labeling restrictions.

QUALITY CHECKING

Telling the quality of matcha from a packet is challenging, but here are a few guidelines:

1 Matcha should always come from Japan, in particular Uji and Nishio (opposite).
2 Look for a recognized brand name.
3 Matcha should come in a high-quality airtight container, whether tins or sachets.
4 The packet should have an organic certification.

If you have bought a top-quality matcha it should be:
- a bright grass—almost neon—green.
- sweet, not at all bitter.
- smooth to the touch, not grainy.

MATCHA PRODUCTION REGIONS

Japan has two "best in show" matcha production areas.

1 Uji is a small city on the southeastern outskirts of Kyoto and is one of the oldest cultural centers in Japan. This area is famed as being the original birthplace of tea in Japan and is renowned for its high-quality green teas. The region is frost-free due to the mild constant winds, and it has perfect growing conditions for matcha production.

2 Nishio lies in Aichi Prefecture and is the largest producer of matcha. For centuries it has been a major tea growing region and has an ideal climate for growing matcha, with a fertile soil and mild, wet weather pattern.

Not only is Nishio the largest producer of matcha green tea, it's also the largest producer of Unagi freshwater eels (unrelated but interesting!).

Uji, Japan

Nishio, Japan

Above Tea bushes growing under shade in Nishio, Japan.

Right Juicy tea leaves ready for plucking in Japan.

MATCHA AROUND THE WORLD

The crucial elements required to produce a great-quality matcha are the growing conditions, the shading, and the grinding (pages 26–7). These have been perfected over the centuries in Japan, where matcha has been so important in the tea ceremony, so we need to look primarily to the Japanese for great matcha.

Around 15 years ago, however, China began to produce larger volumes of ground green tea to compete with the Japanese matcha market. A form of "matcha" is even being produced in Kenya, where it's ground from white tea; and "red matcha" is being ground from Rooibos in South Africa. Although nowadays there's a liberal use of the word "matcha," we really should be thinking of quality shade-grown green tea from Japan when we see the word "matcha."

Matcha Producers Today

The tea industry dominates the countryside in Uji, in Kyoto Prefecture, and in Nishio, in Aichi Prefecture (page 29), the two main tea and matcha producing areas in Japan. The land here looks very different from other tea-growing regions worldwide. Their fields undulate, uninterrupted. Here, roads run sandwiched between verdant green tea fields or less-attractive shaded fields in the spring.

THE MATCHA PRODUCERS

One major player, which manufactures 80 percent of the Japanese matcha in Aichi Prefecture, dominates the producers in Japan. There are also multiple small tea growers in Japan—from tiny family growers with small plots to slightly larger commercial growers. These growers sell their freshly picked "green leaf" to the larger matcha manufacturers, which means that the dominant matcha manufacturers don't exclusively grow all the matcha in Japan.

MATCHA PRODUCTION AS PART OF THE WORLD TEA PRODUCTION

Over five million tons of tea are cropped in the world every year, a mere 3,000 tons of which are produced as matcha in Japan—that means just 0.06 percent of all teas produced globally are sold as matcha.

To make most types of tea you need four kilograms of green leaves to make one kilogram of tea. However, to make one kilogram of ground matcha requires more than six kilograms of fresh green leaves. The extra amount is necessary because the veins and stalks are removed as part of the production process (page 27). This, along with the complex production process, inflates the price of matcha, making it justifiably more expensive than regular tea.

Approximately 2,550 tons of matcha sell each year in Japan, between 85 and 90 percent of the total annual production of matcha. Therefore, only about 10 percent of Japanese matcha is exported, but demand for exported matcha is increasing rapidly.

WHO DRINKS THE MOST MATCHA?

The top five consumers of matcha:

1. *Japan* 2. *USA*
3. *China* 4. *Germany*
5. *UK*

THE CHANGING MATCHA INDUSTRY

The matcha industry has changed considerably since the export market became more established. teapigs was the first company to bring matcha to the UK in 2008, and since then the matcha industry in the UK has flourished. Demand has also grown considerably in other European countries and in the USA and China in particular. It's now common to see matcha on the menu in leading cafés and restaurants around the world (page 49). This has resulted in an increased demand for fine matcha in Japan and for ingredient-grade matcha for use in matcha-flavored food and drinks, which is good news for the producers.

Although most matcha isn't produced organically, the demand for organic matcha has also increased in recent years.

Top Freshly picked tea leaves being steamed.

Bottom left Tencha leaf being ground down on stone grinders to make matcha powder.

Bottom right Sorting the leaves carefully for grading quality.

The Health Benefits

The "superpower" green tea

We all love a cup of delicious, top-quality green tea. Here we will help you to understand why adding our "superpower" green tea to your diet will make you feel a little bit more super!

The secret to matcha is obvious when you start to learn more about this superpower drink. There are two main reasons that matcha is so amazing:

1. **The way it is grown and produced.**
2. **The way it is drunk.**

1 THE POWER OF SHADE

Matcha bushes grow under lots of shade, which boosts the production of amino acids and the chlorophyll content (that's the stuff that makes the leaves their lovely bright-green color). Then the leaves are hand-picked, and all the stems and veins are removed, leaving only the juiciest, most nutrient-rich leaves. The leaves are ground by granite stones to a super-fine powder, which is packed immediately to preserve all the nutrients. See also "The Production of Matcha," page 20.

2 A PACKED CUPPA

That brings us to our second secret—the way matcha is drunk. When you drink regular green tea, whether loose or in a bag, you throw away the leaves after you have let them infuse. This is a bit like boiling spinach, throwing away the spinach and just drinking the water—you will get some of the nutrients, but you're discarding the best bit—the leaves with all the nutrients.

When you drink matcha, you mix the bright-green, nutrient-rich powder into liquid and ingest the entire tea leaf. Every little particle is packed with goodness, so when you knock back your matcha, you're consuming every tiny bit of that lovely green tea.

> **"SHADING THE TEA BUSHES BOOSTS THE AMINO ACID AND CHLOROPHYLL CONTENT; WHILE CONSUMING THE WHOLE LEAF MEANS YOU GET EVERY LITTLE BIT OF MATCHA GOODNESS."**

Matcha's health benefits

Why is matcha so good for you? Why does it make you feel great? Why is it a superb alternative to regular green tea? Why should you swap your favorite cup of the black stuff for this bright-green brew?

GREEN TEA FLAVONOIDS

EGCG is big news. Never heard of it? Matcha contains high amounts of natural green tea flavonoids known as catechins. Epigallocatechin gallate or EGCG (for those, like us, who cannot pronounce its chemical name) is a major catechin. Many of the studies that have investigated the antioxidant power of matcha have focused on how EGCG works within the human body. See also page 38.

Calorie burning

A large number of scientific studies are looking at the effect that green tea may have on the body's thermogenesis—that is, the rate it burns calories—and on its impact upon fat oxidization during exercise (page 39).

Green tea extract is now used in many slimming supplements.

Matcha is probably the purest and most natural form of green tea extract —and lovely to drink, too.

WHAT CAN MATCHA DO FOR YOU?

Dazzling skin

Green tea contains polyphenols, and researchers at the University of Alabama have found that consumption of green tea polyphenols can inhibit UV-radiation-induced skin damage [1].

It's well known that the sun's UV rays can damage skin, cause premature aging, and even cause skin cancer. The study found that these polyphenols can prevent sun-induced skin disorders, helping to keep your skin young and beautiful.

Energy, concentration, and focus

As with all types of green tea, matcha contains caffeine, a natural stimulant. Matcha also contains an important amino acid called L-theanine. These two compounds appear to work together to give a slow release of energy, rather than a quick energy boost and then a dip, and many drinkers report that they feel alert and focused for a number of hours after they consume matcha. Much research has been—and continues to be—conducted into how L-theanine may help promote alpha brain waves, which are known to help with concentration (page 41).

Focus

Matcha is believed to give you a slow release of energy that lasts throughout the day while keeping you calm, alert, and focused at the same time. That's why Japanese students drink it when they're cramming for their exams, and it's also why Buddhist monks have always drunk matcha to help them meditate.

Drinking matcha is like drinking ten cups of regular green tea for its nutrient value—that's why we think matcha is a superpower green tea.

Extra oomph

Lots of athletes are discovering the benefits of drinking matcha while training. Olympic swimmer Rebecca Adlington, for example, is a big matcha fan.

" MATCHA IS AN ALL-NATURAL BEVERAGE THAT HAS BEEN DRUNK FOR CENTURIES FOR ITS AMAZING PROPERTIES. "

The experts' view

We know how amazing matcha is, but don't just take our word for it. We asked top nutritionists and authors of the bestselling book *The Sirtfood Diet*, **Aidan Goggins** and **Glen Matten**, to expand on the varied and notable health benefits of matcha. Both experts in the field of health and nutrition, Aidan is a trained pharmacist and nutritionist, and Glen has a master's degree in nutritional medicine.

A little-known fact is that matcha green tea was Europe's original tea. In the early 1600s, Dutch traders set up in Japan, where matcha was the tea of choice. They sent it to Europe, where it quickly became very popular. However, changes in supply meant a switch to black tea a century later. But with matcha green tea readily available once more, everyone can again enjoy this delicious beverage and all its health-giving wonder by going green.

The reason tea is believed to be so good for us is due primarily to its rich content of a group of powerful plant nutrients called catechins and especially a particular one—epigallocatechin gallate (EGCG) (page 36). Whereas black tea contains only about 3–10 percent catechins, green tea boasts a staggering 30–40 percent, with matcha by far the best green tea catechin source.

In order to appreciate matcha truly, first we need to look at the amazing health benefits of the catechins and EGCG that modern science has unearthed before looking at what marks matcha as the supreme form of green tea.

Look out for the "Our Nutritionists" logos in the recipe section, as these highlight the super-healthy recipes chosen by Aidan and Glen.

GREEN TEA CATECHINS AND HEALTH

Cancer

A large and growing body of laboratory, animal, and human research suggests an important role for green tea in cancer prevention. Significant benefits have been observed for green tea consumption, especially EGCG, for inhibiting cancer growth in the prostate, lungs, stomach, and breasts [1–4].

With benefits for such a broad range of cancers, low toxicity, and easy consumption with low risk of side effects, researchers are looking to green tea as a potential complement to more conventional cancer treatments.

Heart Health

When it comes to matters of the heart, there is much love for green tea.

A 2014 review, which combined the results from 20 trials, found that green tea consumption has significant benefit for lowering blood pressure and cholesterol [5].

But how does that translate to the chances of actually succumbing to heart disease? A large Japanese study of 40,530 adults found that those who enjoyed five cups or more of green tea daily had a 26 percent reduction in death from cardiovascular disease compared to those consuming just one cup a day [6].

Diabetes

There has been considerable interest in the benefits of green tea for diabetes and improving blood sugar control.

In 2013, an analysis of 17 trials put this to the test and found that green tea consumption significantly lowered levels of fasting blood sugar and a measure called HbA1c, which indicates long-term blood sugar levels [7].

The real-world effect of these benefits manifested when researchers pulled together all relevant studies that have looked at the relationship between tea drinking and diabetes risk. The results of this analysis show that drinking more than 3 to 4 cups of green tea a day reduces the risk of type 2 diabetes by around 15–20 percent when compared to non-tea drinkers [8, 9].

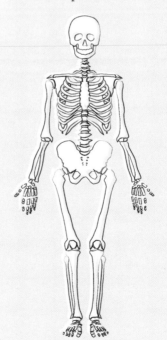

Bone Health

Green tea is also emerging as an invaluable food in the battle against osteoporosis. Early-stage studies show that catechins enhance bone formation and suppress bone breakdown. Studies from countries around the world, including the UK, link tea consumption as a protective factor against osteoporosis.

One early-stage intervention study of 150 post-menopausal women with early stage osteoporosis found that consuming green tea catechins (equivalent to 4 to 6 cups of green tea a day) for six months reduced bone stress, helped to boost bone formation, and improved muscle strength [10].

"WE LIKE TO REFER TO MATCHA AS GREEN TEA ON STEROIDS."

Weight

Green tea has received much hype as a weight loss aid, but what's the science?

Green tea catechins exert a thermogenic effect, which means they help drive fat burning in the body, making it a valuable aid in the battle of the bulge. Habitual green tea drinkers have been shown to have a 20 percent reduction in body fat percentage as well as a favorable reduction in their waist-to-hip ratio [11].

An overall review of the evidence in 2013 found promising results from green tea consumption in improving body composition [12]. Drinking green tea also shows benefits for maintaining fat loss after people stopped dieting as well as in enhancing the fat-burning effects from exercise, making it truly a food for improving body shape.

(References given on page 160.)

Green tea as a wonder Sirtfood

As practising clinicians in the field of nutritional medicine, Aidan and Glen are well versed when it comes to recommending specific foods for treating specific conditions. However, green tea transcends this, so broad are its health benefits. Here they look at matcha's advantages.

In addition to all the conditions discussed on pages 38–9, we could add numerous other benefits to the list relating to infections, arthritis, dental health, immune function, and neurodegeneration. It seems that there are very few people who would not benefit from drinking green tea regularly.

All of this begs the question—how can one food do so much?

It's all down to the fact that green tea, and especially matcha, is one of a newly discovered group of wonder foods called Sirtfoods. These foods contain especially high levels of special nutrients that switch on a master group of wellbeing genes that exist in all of us, called sirtuins.

When our sirtuins turn on, they activate a recycling process in our cells that clears out the cellular debris and clutter that accumulates over time, causing ill health and loss of vitality. To fuel this recycling process, the body uses our fat cells. The result of activating our sirtuin genes means we increase our sense of wellbeing, we boost our resistance to disease, and we burn significant amounts of fat in the process. Activating sirtuins has been shown to be a key factor in preventing the many chronic diseases that afflict us, explaining why green tea has such wide-ranging benefits in these conditions.

Until now, the benefits of foods have been judged on the basis of their content of vitamins, minerals, antioxidants, and other nutrients that nourish the body. The discovery of Sirtfoods has changed all this.

Sirtuins aren't turned on through nourishment though; in fact, the opposite is the case. They turn on only when the cells in our body are stressed. Indeed, the reason green tea is so good for us is that the catechins (especially EGCG) act like weak toxins that stress the cells in our body.

At first thought, the idea that stress or toxins could be good for us might seem odd, but bear with us.

What we're talking about is a controlled, physiological stress, caused by these natural plant compounds. This low-level "stress" switches on our sirtuin genes, which ramp up the efficiency of our cells, causing them to adapt to the stress and become fitter, healthier, and more resilient to future stresses. By repeated exposure to this low-level stress, our bodies become increasingly stronger and ultimately more resilient to declining health and disease.

Only certain plant foods have these nutrients in sufficient quantities to class them as Sirtfoods. As well as matcha, other examples of top Sirtfoods include kale, arugula, parsley, red onions, strawberries, walnuts, turmeric, and cocoa. Because the nutrients in these foods work synergistically, they make great additions to your diet alongside regular consumption of matcha. See the recipe section from page 50 for a wealth of matcha-rich recipes.

Why is matcha so special?

Glen and Aidan like to refer to matcha as "green tea on steroids!" Here they outline how matcha smashes standard green tea in terms of its catechin content and especially its level of the much prized EGCG.

One of the frequent findings in green tea research is that to realize the benefits of EGCG and the catechins fully, we need to drink multiple cups of green tea a day. But the absorption of EGCG can be hindered when consumed with certain foods, so to get the maximum benefit we might need to drink amounts of green tea that aren't practical for many people.

This leads us to the beauty of matcha, which is its potency—you don't need to drink lots to gain the health benefits. Matcha is also a fantastic ingredient for cooking, so it's the answer for anyone who wants to reap all the benefits of green tea in the easiest and most convenient way. See the recipe section from page 50 for a wealth of ideas on how to include matcha in your daily diet.

But wait, there's an added bonus, too. Tea is one of only a few plants that contains L-theanine, and matcha green tea has the advantage of being grown in the shade, which means it produces even more L-theanine than standard green tea. L-theanine promotes a mentally relaxed state, reduces nervous system stress, and helps stop the mind from racing (page 36).

The combination of catechins, low-dose caffeine, and L-theanine makes matcha green tea the perfect source of focused energy.

MAXING UP YOUR MATCHA

When it comes to green tea, there can be little doubt that matcha reigns supreme. But to get the maximum bang for your buck and help you on your way, we've put together our top matcha tips:

OPTIMIZING YOUR MATCHA INTAKE

1 *Opt for organic matcha, which typically contains higher amounts of healthful catechins.*

2 *When making tea, use hot but not boiling water (page 52) to maintain the integrity of the matcha catechins. Off the boil, around 176°F/80°C is perfect.*

3 *Add a squeeze of lemon juice for its natural acidity that helps to increase the absorption of beneficial green tea compounds.*

4 *Try to drink your matcha tea at least an hour before or two hours after eating food, which will mean you absorb higher amounts of EGCG.*

Matcha Today

Modern matcha

Matcha is an integral part of the culinary experience and social life of Japan. The Japanese incorporate matcha as an ingredient into an amazingly diverse range of drinks and foods. Not only does it have numerous health advantages (see "The Health Benefits," page 32), but its unique flavor can make even the most bland food interesting.

As soon as matcha and its umami taste (opposite) became popular in Japan it became an important ingredient in Japanese cuisine. With a distinctive taste, matcha is a high-end flavor to add to anything and everything.

While we understand the long religious significance behind matcha (see "The History of Matcha," page 8), and ceremonial-grade matcha is traditionally used for the Japanese tea ceremony (page 14), most of the matcha consumed today is enjoyed for its taste and health benefits.

The rest of the world is now embracing the wonderful, all-natural bright-green brilliance of matcha. There is nothing more satisfying than opening a tin in front of someone who has never experienced matcha before—the puff of green powder always gets a "wow!" People are embracing it far beyond the blend of matcha and hot water—adding it to everything from lattes and cocktails to salads and stir-fries.

Nowadays matcha travels all around the world—see page 49 for the best bars, cafés, and restaurants to enjoy matcha in. Matcha is also used (and some may think abused!) in all kinds of recipes. See the recipe section from page 50 for how to include matcha in your daily diet.

DRINKING MATCHA AT HOME

First things first—respect the tradition of matcha. While you may not have all the gear (page 18), whisking matcha into hot water can be done easily at home.

HOW TO DRINK MATCHA ANY TIME, ANYWHERE

Matcha is incredibly versatile. You can drink it as a hot tea, but you can also add it to fruit juices, smoothies, milk, or even a cocktail. See Drinks from page 54 for a wide range of great ideas. It's so easy to get your matcha hit!

1 *Take ½ teaspoon of matcha.*
2 *Add to your chosen liquid—hot or cold water, milk, fruit juice, or smoothie, etc.*
3 *Blend it and enjoy.*

On the go?
Add a matcha sachet to your drink bottle, shake, and drink!

WHAT IS UMAMI?

We all know about the four basic distinct flavors: sweet, sour, bitter, and salty, but umami is the fifth main flavor. The Japanese chemist Kikunae Ikeda combined "umai" meaning "delicious," with "mi," the word for "taste," to form "umami." Umami has a delicious, savory taste and can be found in foods such as Parmesan cheese, tomatoes, and soy sauce as well as in matcha.

JUST REMEMBER...

Matcha as an ingredient works particularly well with creamy, indulgent flavors. If you are enjoying matcha just for its health benefits, the matcha goodness may be compromised if you enjoy it in an indulgent, cream-topped form!

MATCHA AS A FOOD

Matcha as a drink is only the beginning—because it's a powder you can add it to yogurt, cakes, desserts, soups, any number of different foods. We have given you lots of ideas for creating your own matcha meals (page 50 onward).

MATCHA FOR ANY MEAL

Matcha is everywhere—and in everything—in Japan. But beyond Japan, the taste for matcha has grown over the last ten or so years, and you can enjoy matcha around the world now. US sales alone increased more than 50 percent in 2014 as the "matcha wave" began to take off.

Below are some of our favorite matcha drinks and foods.

MATCHA ICE CREAM

This is delicious if made with top-quality matcha. We love the creaminess and vivid green color of our Coconut and matcha ice cream (page 151); or try the Matcha mochi ice cream balls (page 155) for a taste of Japan at home.

Worth a visit: Japan Ice OUCA, 1F, Ebisu, Shibuya-ku, Tokyo, 150-0013, Japan. (www.ice-ouca.com)
Tombo Japanese Café and Matcha Bar, 29 Thurloe Place, London SW7 2HQ, England. (www.tombocafe.com)

MATCHA CAKES AND DESSERTS

Sweet little treats can be found all over Japan, where bright-green matcha jellies and indulgent cakes are common. Why not try our Mini matcha cheesecakes (page 142) or the Matcha breakfast muffins (page 76).

Worth a visit: Chachanoma, 1st flr, Omotesando SK Bldg, 5–13–14 Jingumae, Tokyo, Japan. Kinozen, Kinozen Bldg, 1–12 Kagurazaka, Shinjuku Ward, Tokyo, Japan.

MATCHA PASTRIES

As the Western diet and the Japanese diet merge, green matcha pastries have emerged. What

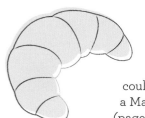

could be nicer than a Matcha croissant (page 78) or indulgent Matcha ring doughnuts (page 132)?

Worth a visit: Sadaharu Aoki is a Japanese pastry chef who lives in Paris, France, and has created numerous matcha-based treats. He has a number of shops in Tokyo, Japan (www.sadaharuaoki.jp) and in Paris, France (www.sadaharuaoki.com).

Aki Boulanger, a specialist French-Japanese bakery, is at 16 rue Sainte-Anne, 75001, Paris, France (www.akiboulanger.com).

MATCHA LATTE

The matcha latte is one of our favorites (see recipes on page 58), and we recommend it to all the cafés we supply matcha to.

Worth a visit: Starbucks has a number of matcha-themed drinks—both juices and hot drinks—on their menu. These are a long way from the bamboo whisk and porcelain bowl but are worth trying (www.starbucks.com).

Bibble and Sip, 253 W. 51st St., New York, NY 10019, USA. (www.bibbleandsip.com)

MATCHA BEER

Enjoy green beer, including a number of matcha-based beers, plus interesting food in the matcha beer garden in the Green Tea Restaurant.

Worth a visit: Green Tea Restaurant, 3-4 Kanda Surugadai, 1F Hotel, Chiyoda 101-0062, Tokyo, Japan.

WEIRD ... OR WONDERFULLY GREEN?

Matcha popcorn, Oreos, Popsicles, or truffles, anyone? Here are some interesting matcha-infused treats.

Matcha potato chips

Salt and vinegar, cheese and onion, or matcha potato chips? Which do you fancy? The largest Japanese snack food maker, Koikeya, has sourced a fine matcha from Uji and infused it into their potato chips to make a high-end Japanese snack.

Matcha on toast

Although some people may find the distinctive green color of matcha bread slightly unnerving, Verde, a Japanese food company, has invented a bright-green matcha-and-milk spread to go on your bright-green toast. Delicious.

Matcha booze

We all love a cocktail blended with matcha (see our Matchatini and Matcha mint fizz cocktails on page 66). In Japan you can buy matcha sake, the ultimate Japanese drink. The matcha is infused at the point of production so the sake has a very strong matcha flavor. New to the market is Kahluha and matcha, one to try (perhaps!).

Matcha Kit Kats

Matcha and chocolate are a wonderful combination, and matcha Kit Kats are just outstanding.

WHERE TO EXPERIENCE THE TEA CEREMONY

For many people, experiencing the tea ceremony while on a visit to Japan is a highlight of their trip. Most of the tea houses given here lie in Kyoto, the traditional home of the tea ceremony, but with careful research you can find tea houses all over Japan where you'll be able to experience an authentic tea ceremony.

Camellia, Kyoto

This super-calm tea house, located on Ninenzaka steps between Gion and Kiyomizu Temple, is in one of Kyoto's most popular areas for sightseeing. A great place to experience a mesmerizing ceremony. 349 Masuya-cho, Kyoto-shi, Kyoto. (www.facebook.com/camellia.kyoto)

En, Kyoto

Learn all about the traditions of the tea ceremony in this small, relaxed tea house. Group and private ceremonies available. 272 Matsubara-cho, Higashiyama-ku, Kyoto. (www.teaceremonyen.com)

Hotel Chinzanso, Tokyo

Set amid the bustle of Tokyo, this "urban oasis" has tranquil and historic tea rooms set in the middle of a stunning garden, which blooms all year round. We recommend the tea ceremony lead by the hotel's resident tea master. 10-8, Sekiguchi 2-chome, Bunkyo-ku, Tokyo 112-8680. (www.hotel-chinzanso-tokyo.com)

Okitsu Club, Kyoto

This is a premium tea house experience! With a vast garden, two tea rooms, an incense ceremony room, and a wide range of ceremonies in English, this is top-quality. Kodokan, 524-1 Mototsuchimikado-cho, Shinmachi, Kamigyo-ku, Kyoto. (www.okitsu-kyoto.com)

Ran Hotei, Kyoto

Set in a 100-year-old Kyoto townhouse, this elegant tea house lies just ten minutes south of Nijo Castle. Experience the ceremony with Canadian tea master Randy Channell Soei at this exquisite tea house and gallery. 64 Kamikawara, Sanjo Omiya, Kyoto. (www.ranhotei.com)

Tea Ceremony Room Ju-An, Kyoto

Just ten minutes from Kyoto Station, this authentic tea house is the real deal. Located in an architectural gem in historic Kyoto, this elegant tea house is set in a typical Japanese garden. Here you can learn all about the rituals of the ceremony and practise the Japanese tea ceremony with an English-speaking host. 508 Shiokojicho, Shimogyo Ward, Kyoto. (www.teaceremonykyoto.com)

Tondaya, Kyoto

This atmospheric tea house is located in an ancient merchant house, or machiya. Tondaya was registered as a National Cultural Heritage site in 1999 and is a lifestyle museum. As well as experiencing the tea ceremony, you can hire kimonos, take a tour of the historic building, and learn all about traditional Japanese arts such as calligraphy and origami. Ichijo-agaru Omiya, Kamigyo-ku Kyoto. (www.tondaya.co.jp/english)

THE BEST OF MATCHA WORLDWIDE

Matcha has been a feature on menus in hipster cafés and Japanese restaurants outside Japan for some time. It's now present on the menus of some mainstream chains, and a number of dedicated matcha bars are opening up outside Japan. These are great places to experiment with matcha creations. See below for where to experience the best of matcha around the world.

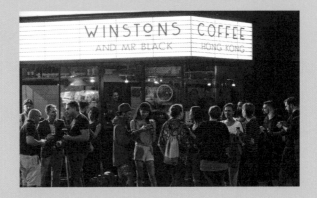

Australia

Chanoma is an authentic, Japanese-style café in central Sydney, providing a delicious selection of matcha drinks—from floats to frappés—as well as a traditional-modern Japanese menu.
Shop 11, 501 George Street, Sydney. (www.chanoma.com.au)
Little Rogue is a coffee house featuring matcha lattes and amazing latte art.
12 Drewery Lane, Melbourne, Victoria 3000. (www.facebook.com/LittleRogueMelbourne)

Canada

Uncle Tetsu's Japanese Matcha Café is a vibrant café featuring a wide range of smoothies, bright-green desserts, and sweet treats on its menu. Famous for the Uncle Tetsu matcha cheesecake.
596 Bay Street, Toronto, Ontario M5G 1M5. (www.uncletetsu.ca)

Germany

This German version of the American café chain **House of Small Wonder** (right) opened in Berlin in December 2014. With numerous Japanese influences, the menu features matcha heavily, while the matcha cappucino is something else!
Johannisstraße 20, 10117 Berlin. (www.houseofsmallwonder.de)

Hong Kong

Winstons Coffee (*pictured above*) is a popular recent addition to the matcha coffee scene. Try a matcha latte with a matcha egg tart—delicious! Fu Kwok Building, 213 Queen's Rd W, Sai Ying Pun. (www.facebook.com/winstonscoffeehk)

Sinagpore

With over 150 years of history and three shops in central Singapore, **Tsujiri** serves the most amazing matcha ice cream desserts, along with a wide range of hot matcha beverages.
6 Eu Tong Sen Street #01-74 The Central Singapore 059817. (www.tsujiri.sg)

UK

Laveli Bakery in West London serves great matcha smoothies.
104 Askew Road, Shepherds Bush, London W12 9BL. (www.lavelibakery.com)
Moksha Caffe was an early adopter of the matcha trend and is one of our favorite stockists. We thank you!
4–5 York Place, Brighton, BN1 4GU. (www.mokshacaffe.com)

USA

Matcha Bar NYC is well worth a visit. They have a range of matcha drinks and eats available.
93 Wythe Ave, Brooklyn, NY 11249. (www.matchabarnyc.com)
Matcha Box has a good range of hot and cold matcha drinks and food.
8036 W 3rd St, Los Angeles, CA 90048. (www.matchabox.com).
House of Small Wonder (HSOW) is a very popular place for breakfast, brunch, lunch, and pastries. Focusing on quality rather than quantity, this café chain uses matcha as a key ingredient.
77 N 6th Street, Brooklyn, NY 11211. (www.houseofsmallwonder.com)

Matcha Recipes

Choosing, storing, and preparing matcha

Matcha is a wonderful ingredient, but not all matcha is the same. Like most foods and drinks, there's a wide range available. See below for what to seek in top-quality matcha and how to look after it once you have purchased it.

Look
You want a bright-green, rich, fresh-looking powder. This indicates that the stems and veins have been removed, and only the quality "fleshy" parts of the leaves have been used.

Smell
Giving the matcha a good sniff tells you the quality of the matcha—a sweet, vegetable, fresh smell means good stuff!

Taste
A good-quality matcha tastes good. It's as simple as that. It should have a thick, sweet, umami taste (page 45) with no astringency or bitterness. While the taste of matcha itself is unusual, it should never be unpleasant.

Touch
If you compare a quality matcha with a low-grade green tea powder, you can feel the difference. Pour out a small pile of each powder onto some paper. Press your finger into each and drag it outward (like you're finger painting). The good-quality matcha feels like face cream—thick and smooth. The green tea powder will feel more grainy and dry.

Appearance
The matcha should be a rich, bright, deep green color when brewed.

Storage
Now that you have invested in the finest matcha, make sure you look after it. Matcha is processed in a cool, dark room to keep it super fresh, so storing it in a cool, dark place, such as the fridge, is ideal.

Light isn't great for matcha, so put the lid on quickly after you have taken the matcha out of its container. If the matcha isn't going to be consumed for a while, store it in the freezer.

HOW TO MAKE MATCHA THE TRADITIONAL WAY

The classic way to make matcha tea is to whisk it into hot water using a bamboo whisk, then serve it in a bowl, as the Japanese do.

Alternatively, although not quite as authentic, you can use a handheld blender or milk frother if you don't have a bamboo whisk.

POW

1 Add about ½ teaspoon of matcha to your bowl.

2 Add a small amount of warm (but not boiling) water. If the water is too hot, it will burn the leaves.

3 Whisk the matcha and water together using a bamboo whisk.

4 Top with more warm water and enjoy straight away.

The matcha challenge

We've heard all about matcha's superpowers, and lots of people tell us how drinking matcha has made them feel more energized and focused.

Every year, we invite people to take the matcha challenge. Drink matcha every day for two weeks and see how sprightly you feel. The results are always amazing. In 2016, 700 people took part, and 81 percent said they felt more energized.

If you'd like to give it a go, we've put together this calendar to help you; or check out the recipes that follow. With so many ways to enjoy matcha, it shouldn't be too tricky a challenge!

THE MATCHA CHALLENGE CALENDAR

DAY 1
Welcome to the first day of the matcha challenge.

Enjoy a Glorious green or Beautiful berry juice (page 56) for a healthy start.

DAY 2
POW

Start the day properly with Matcha eggs Florentine (page 82) or Matcha granola with berries (page 74).

DAY 3
Unlike coffee, you won't get a rush of energy and then a crash with matcha. It's all about slow release.

Relax and enjoy a cup of matcha tea mid-morning.

DAY 4
99%
of people would recommend matcha to a friend.

Raw matcha coconut fudge bites (page 96) are ideal for sharing with friends.

DAY 5
Enjoy a tea break with a friend.

Whip up an Almond matcha latte or a White chocolate matcha latte (page 58).

DAY 6
In a rush? Take your matcha on the go.

Simply add matcha to your water bottle, shake, and drink!

DAY 7
yay!

You're halfway through. Treat time!

Matcha blondies (page 130) are decadent and delicious.

DAY 8

Matcha is so versatile that you can enjoy it at any meal.

Matcha poached salmon, brocolli, and chickpea salad (page 102) makes a perfect power-packed lunch.

DAY 9
81%
of people felt more energized after having matcha for two weeks.

Our Hazelnut and vanilla smoothie (page 70) is packed with flavor and goodness.

DAY 10
Matcha for dinner? Why not?!

Chicken, turmeric, matcha, and pepper one-pot meal (page 116) is wonderfully spicy.

DAY 11
Matcha tastes great with citrus. Try:

A refreshing Matcha lemonade (page 64).

DAY 12

Healthy breakfast!

Try our yummy Matcha overnight oats (page 72).

DAY 13
One day to go— it's matcha cocktail time!

What do you fancy? A Matchatini or a zingy Matcha mint fizz cocktail (page 66)?

DAY 14
Yay! You have completed the matcha challenge . . .

Coconut and matcha cupcakes (page 129) . . . it is a celebration after all!

6 Drinks

Matcha juices

We teamed up with nutritionists Aidan Goggins and Glen Matten to create some super-healthy recipes, including two of these delicious juices. Here they tell us why these juices are so great for you.

To make these vibrant juices, simply place all the ingredients in a blender and blend until smooth. Serve immediately over ice.

Peach and apple juice

This juice is sweet and summery, and the Greek yogurt makes it feel indulgent.

SERVES 1

1 peach, peeled
½ cup (100ml) apple juice
1 tbsp Greek yogurt
½ tsp matcha powder
squeeze of honey
ice, to serve

Beautiful berry juice

SUPER-HEALTHY

"We love berries and their bumper supply of healthful anthocyanins, the pigments that give berries their color and have potent benefits in warding off obesity, diabetes, and heart disease, as well as boosting bone density and brain health."

SERVES 1

5 large strawberries
10 raspberries
10 blueberries
½ cup (100ml) apple juice

5 mint leaves
2 sprigs of basil
½ tsp matcha powder
ice, to serve

Glorious green juice

SUPER-HEALTHY

"Go green with the brassica queen! Packed with vitamins C, K, and folate as well as polyphenols and immune-boosting beta-carotene, kale is a nutrient powerhouse, which when combined with matcha makes for a health blockbuster. The addition of banana gives it an irresistible creaminess."

SERVES 1

1 banana
2 handfuls of kale
juice of 1 lime
½ cup (100ml) apple juice
½ tsp matcha powder
ice, to serve

Almond matcha latte

One of our favorite drinks, this is equally delicious made with hazelnut milk, coconut milk, or soy milk. If using cow milk, choose skim rather than whole so the matcha flavor comes through better.

SERVES 1

½ tsp matcha powder
hot water
squeeze of agave syrup
½ tsp ground cinnamon
½ tsp ground nutmeg
¼ tsp vanilla powder
1¼ cups (300ml) unsweetened
   almond milk

1 Put the matcha powder in a mug and add a little hot (but not boiling) water. Whisk, blend, or froth to make a paste. We use a small handheld electric whisk.

2 Add the agave syrup, cinnamon, nutmeg, and vanilla powder and stir or whisk again.

3 Heat the almond milk and whisk to make frothy. A handheld whisk works well, or if you have an espresso machine with a steamer, you can use that.

4 Add the milk to the matcha paste and enjoy the yumminess!

Note
This is amazing iced. Make a paste with a little cold almond milk (instead of hot water), add the agave and spices, and top with more almond milk and ice.

White chocolate matcha latte

Matcha tastes simply amazing with white chocolate, and this tasty latte is perfect for an indulgent treat. Add a slice of Chocolate layer cake with matcha frosting (page 124) or a Matcha macaron (page 134), and you'll be in matcha heaven.

SERVES 1

½ cup (100ml) heavy whipping cream
1 oz (30g) white chocolate
¾ cup (200ml) milk
¼ tsp vanilla powder
½ tsp matcha powder, plus extra for garnish

1 Whip the cream and set aside.

2 Melt the white chocolate in a saucepan with the milk and vanilla powder.

3 Add the matcha powder to the saucepan, whisk until smooth, then pour into a mug.

4 Pile the whipped cream on top of the latte.

5 Add a sprinkling of matcha powder for fun and color!

Dairy-free almond and matcha frappé

Almonds and matcha are a great combination in this refreshing frappé. Make sure you use a good-quality almond milk with no added sugar, and you'll get a delicate sweetness from the almonds as well as the burst of matcha goodness.

SERVES 1

¾ cup (200ml) almond milk
½ tsp matcha powder
¼ tsp vanilla powder
2 ice cubes, plus extra for serving

1 Add the almond milk, matcha powder, vanilla powder, and 2 ice cubes to a blender.

2 Blend until smooth, then pour over ice and serve immediately.

Matcha coconut teashake

You can make this super-simple teashake with any ice cream you fancy, but our favorite flavors are coconut, vanilla, or ginger. The coconut flakes on top make this even yummier. For the ultimate drink, use white chocolate sprinkles.

SERVES 1

½ cup (100ml) skim milk
2–3 scoops of good-quality coconut ice cream
1 tsp matcha powder
coconut milk, to thin the consistency, if desired
coconut flakes (optional)

1 Put the milk and ice cream into a blender and blend together.

2 Add the matcha powder and blend again.

3 Depending on how thick you like it, add more coconut milk and blend again until you reach the desired thickness.

4 Pour into a glass, sprinkle with coconut flakes if you wish, drink, and grin!

White chocolate and matcha milkshake

Yum, yum, yum! Creamy vanilla and white chocolate mixed with matcha are an indulgent and dreamy combination. Dress it up or down as you wish, varying the decoration depending on your mood.

SERVES 1

½ cup (100ml) heavy whipping
    cream
1 oz (25g) white chocolate chips,
    plus extra for garnish
½ tsp vanilla sugar
1¼ cups (300ml) skim milk
½ tsp matcha powder
squeeze of honey

1 Whip the cream and set aside.

2 Melt the chocolate chips in a saucepan over low heat.

3 Mix the vanilla sugar into the milk.

4 Add the milk, matcha, and honey to the melted chocolate mixture and blend or whisk.

5 Pour into a glass. Garnish with the whipped cream and chocolate chips and serve immediately.

Vanilla matcha milkshake

This guilt-free, dairy-free milkshake tastes lovely and creamy and is packed with goodness from the matcha, banana, and almond milk. For variety, experiment with other kinds of milk—we particularly like coconut milk.

SERVES 1

1 banana, frozen
½ cup (115ml) unsweetened
    almond milk
½ tsp matcha powder
½ tsp vanilla powder, plus extra
    for garnish
2 handfuls of ice cubes,
    plus 1 handful to serve
1 tsp honey

1 Add all the ingredients to a blender and blend until smooth.

2 Serve with a sprinkling of vanilla powder and a handful of ice cubes.

Matcha lemonade

This is one of our favorite lunchtime drinks, created one hot summer's day in Brooklyn, New York. With lots of lemon, agave, and matcha, this is a wonderfully zesty and fresh tonic.

SERVES 1

½ tsp matcha powder
squeeze of agave syrup
juice of 1 lemon
¾ cup (200ml) seltzer or club soda
handful of ice cubes, to serve
4 mint leaves for garnish

1 In a pitcher, mix the matcha powder and agave syrup into a paste.

2 Once dissolved, add the lemon juice and water.

3 Stir well, then pour into a tall glass filled with ice, and garnish with mint leaves.

Matcha mint iced tea

This is a great green tea pick-me-up at the end of a long day. It's refreshing, sparkly, and sophisticated. Add a splash of rum for a grown-up version.

SERVES 1

¾ cup (200ml) water or seltzer
½ tsp matcha powder
juice of 1 lime
handful of mint leaves
squeeze of honey
handful of ice cubes, to serve

1 Put the water or seltzer, matcha powder, lime, mint, and honey into a blender. Blend until smooth.

2 Pour into a glass filled with ice and serve.

Matcha cocktails

The teapigs' team worked hard as mixologists to come up with these inventive and incredibly tasty green cocktails.

Matchatini

A vibrant twist on a classic and well-loved cocktail, the Grand Marnier complements the matcha perfectly in this elegant cocktail.

SERVES 1

½ tsp matcha powder
1½ tbsp (25ml) Grand Marnier
3 tbsp (50ml) vodka
4–5 ice cubes

1 Put all the ingredients into a cocktail shaker. Shake well then strain.

2 Pour into a chilled martini glass and enjoy.

Matcha citrus cocktail

Super tasty and slightly tart, this cocktail is perfect for a warm summer evening.

SERVES 1

2 scoops of lemon sorbet
1½ tbsp (25ml) gin
½ cup (115ml) ginger ale
4–5 mint leaves, chopped, plus extra for garnish
juice of 1 lemon
½ tsp matcha powder

1 Place all the ingredients in a blender and blend until smooth.

2 Pour into a chilled cocktail glass, garnish with mint leaves, and serve.

Matcha mint fizz

Summer in a flute—this makes a great alternative to a classic Bellini or Kir Royale. Perfect for a celebratory drink, it packs a healthy punch.

SERVES 1

8 mint leaves
½ tsp matcha powder
1 tsp agave syrup
juice of 1 lime
scant ½ cup (100ml) chilled champagne

1 In a blender, pulverize the mint with the matcha powder, agave syrup, and lime juice.

2 Pour in the champagne slowly. Stir gently until mixed well.

3 Pour into a champagne glass and serve chilled.

7 Breakfast

Matcha smoothies

SUPER-HEALTHY

Here are four delicious smoothies—great at any time of the day, but especially at breakfast—with notes from Aidan and Glen that explain what makes them so healthy!

To make these nutritious smoothies, simply place all the ingredients in a blender (except the chocolate in the Hazelnut and vanilla smoothie), adding the matcha last. Blend until smooth, pour into glasses, and serve straight away.

Hazelnut and vanilla smoothie

"Bursting with skin-nourishing cocoa flavanols and omega-3, this smoothie is specially designed to make you beautiful from the inside out."

SERVES 2

1 cup (250ml) hazelnut milk
2 tbsp natural yogurt
6 strawberries, quartered
1 tsp flax seeds
½ tsp vanilla powder
1 tsp matcha powder
3 ice cubes (optional)

GARNISH
2 tsp plain chocolate shavings
(85% cocoa solids)

Coconut breakfast smoothie

Our nutritionists suggest adding plain chocolate for a boost of cocoa flavanols.

SERVES 2

1 cup (200ml) coconut milk
2 tbsp coconut yogurt
1 banana, sliced, plus extra for garnish
1 tsp matcha powder

Dairy-free smoothie

"Creamy heaven—this smoothie is a delicious way to boost your intake of plant goodness! It's quick and easy to make your own fresh almond milk (see below), and almonds and matcha share many similar health benefits, making them a perfect pairing."

SERVES 2

1⅔ cups (400ml) unsweetened almond
milk (see below)
3 dates
½ avocado
1 tsp matcha powder
3 ice cubes (optional)

HOMEMADE ALMOND MILK
Soak 1 cup (145g) blanched almonds overnight to soften them. In the morning, rinse well and blend in a high-powered blender with 2 cups (500ml) water.

The green smoothie

"Experience matcha goodness in its ultimate form. The natural acids in the lemon juice help to enhance the absorption of EGCG. Best enjoyed on an empty stomach, this is a great smoothie to start any day."

SERVES 2

1 oz (25g) kale
½ oz (10g) arugula
1 apple, cored and chopped
1 pear, cored and chopped
juice of 1 lemon

1¾ cups (400ml) coconut milk
1 tsp matcha powder
3 ice cubes (optional)

Matcha overnight oats

SUPER-HEALTHY

We worked with our nutritionists to devise this hearty breakfast that combines oats, apples, nuts, and matcha—four key foods that "help to lower cholesterol levels and slash the risk of heart disease."

SERVES 2

FOR THE OATS
1 cup (80g) rolled oats
2 tsp chia seeds
1½ cups (375ml) almond milk
    (or hazelnut, rice, or oat milk)
1 tsp matcha powder
2 pinches of ground cinnamon
1 tsp runny honey

FOR THE TOPPING
1 apple, peeled, cored, and
    chopped
1 tsp pumpkin seeds
handful of mixed nuts

1 If you have time make this in advance—ideally the night before you wish to eat it. Place the oats and chia seeds in a bowl or container.

2 In a separate bowl or jar, add 1 tbsp of the almond milk to the matcha powder and whisk to make a smooth paste. Top with the rest of the milk and mix well.

3 Pour the matcha milk mixture over the oats, then stir in the cinnamon and honey. Cover and refrigerate overnight.

4 When ready to eat, transfer the oats to two bowls and top with the chopped apple, pumpkin seeds, and nuts.

Matcha yogurt with blueberry compote

SUPER-HEALTHY

"We're making no bones about it: this combo is designed to give your skeletal health a big boost. We need sufficient calcium for healthy bones, and research shows that natural plant compounds have a dramatic benefit too, with berries, prunes, and green tea being three leading contenders."

SERVES 2

½ cup (50g) blueberries
4 prunes, chopped
1 tsp matcha powder
2 cups (500ml) natural yogurt
1 tsp vanilla extract
handful of flaked almonds
*   for garnish*

1 To make the compote, place the blueberries and prunes in a small saucepan and cover with water.

2 Bring to a boil then simmer, stirring continuously until all the water has evaporated and you have a compote/jelly consistency. Set aside to cool.

3 To make the matcha yogurt, add the matcha powder to 2 tbsp of the yogurt and whisk to make a paste. Add the remaining yogurt and the vanilla extract and stir well.

4 Once the compote is cool, transfer it into two glasses or bowls, top with the yogurt and flaked almonds, and enjoy.

Matcha granola with berries

SUPER HEALTHY

This is a fantastic breakfast for sustained energy because the oats provide slow-releasing energy. Aidan and Glen devised this recipe after exciting research showed that natural compounds found in berries, green tea, and cinnamon have the ability to promote healthy blood sugar and insulin levels.

SERVES 4

2 tbsp coconut oil
1 cup (100g) rolled oats
½ cup (80g) mixed nuts
  (cashews, pistachios,
  almonds, pecans, etc.),
  chopped
1 tbsp pumpkin seeds
1 tbsp sesame seeds
1 tbsp matcha powder
½ tsp ground cinnamon
3 tbsp runny honey
1¾ cups (400g) Greek yogurt
1 cup (140g) strawberries, halved
  or quartered
⅔ cup (100g) blueberries

1 Preheat the oven to 325°F/160°C. Line a baking sheet with baking parchment.

2 To make the granola, heat the coconut oil gently in a saucepan until it melts. Remove from the heat and stir in the oats, nuts, and seeds. Add the matcha powder, cinnamon, and honey and mix together well.

3 Spread the granola mixture evenly over the lined baking sheet and bake for 15 minutes, turning it 2–3 times, until crisp and toasted.

4 Remove from the oven and cool thoroughly before storing in an airtight container.

5 To serve, layer the yogurt, granola, and berries in glass dishes, jars, or pots.

VARIATIONS
• Experiment with other seasonal berries, such as blackberries or redcurrants, or try dried cranberries, blueberries, or Goji berries.
• Add any of the following to the granola mix: sunflower or flax seeds, chopped dried figs or raisins, desiccated or dry shredded coconut, chopped Brazils or walnuts, or vanilla extract.
• This granola also tastes delicious with almond milk and fresh fruit.

Matcha breakfast muffins

These muffins are hearty, oaty, and very satisfying at breakfast. For a snack version, add white or plain chocolate chips when you mix in the nuts, stirring them in gently.

MAKES 12 MUFFINS

1 cup (100g) rolled oats
2 cups (200g) all-purpose flour
2 tsp baking powder
1 tsp baking soda
1 tbsp matcha powder
¼ tsp sea salt
½ cup (85g) light brown sugar
4 large ripe bananas
1 large egg, beaten
½ cup (60g) melted butter
  (or light olive oil)
¾ cup (85g) chopped walnuts
  or pecans

1 Preheat the oven to 350°F/180°C and line a 12-hole muffin pan with cupcake liners.

2 In a large bowl, combine the oats, flour, baking powder, baking soda, matcha powder, salt, and sugar. Mix together and make a well in the center.

3 Mash the bananas with a fork in another bowl. Stir in the beaten egg and melted butter (or olive oil). Add to the dry mixture with the walnuts or pecans and fold through until just combined—take care not to over-mix. If the mixture seems too thick or a little dry, add a little orange juice or milk to thin it.

4 Spoon the mixture into the cupcake liners and bake for 20–25 minutes until the muffins have risen and a toothpick inserted in the middle comes out clean.

5 Serve the muffins warm or cold. They can be kept fresh in an airtight container stored in a cool place for 2–3 days.

VARIATIONS

- You can flavor the muffins with a few drops of vanilla extract or add a little ground cinnamon, ginger, and nutmeg for a spicy result.
- Mix in some freshly grated orange zest and the juice of 1 orange.
- For more fiber and texture, try stirring a tablespoon of flax seeds into the mixture or sprinkle the tops with pumpkin seeds before baking.

Matcha croissants

When we first heard you could get matcha croissants, we thought "Wow!" These look and taste amazing—deliciously buttery with a lovely, smooth matcha taste.

MAKES ABOUT 12 CROISSANTS

5 cups (500g) strong white bread flour, plus extra for dusting
1 tbsp matcha powder
2 tsp salt
¼ cup (60g) superfine sugar

2 sachets fast-action dried yeast
1¼ cups (300ml) cool water
2½ sticks (300g) unsalted butter, chilled
1 egg, beaten for glazing

1 Put the flour, matcha powder, salt, sugar, and yeast in a large mixing bowl. Make a well in the center and gradually add the cool water, stirring well between additions.

2 When it's all added and mixed, take out the ball of dough and knead on a lightly floured work surface for about 10 minutes, until the dough is stiff. Use the ball of your hand to push the dough away from you and stretch it before pulling it back and squashing it into a ball. Give it a quarter-turn, then repeat. Don't be gentle—really stretch and knead it hard to make it elastic. Alternatively, you can use a stand mixer with a dough hook attachment.

3 Place the dough in a lightly oiled bowl, cover with plastic wrap or put in a plastic bag, and chill in the fridge for 1–2 hours.

4 Put the butter between 2 sheets of baking parchment and, using a rolling pin, bash it until you have a large rectangle, about 8 x 6 in (20 x 15cm).

5 On a lightly floured surface, roll out the chilled dough to a large rectangle, about 16 x 8 in (40 x 20cm). Place the butter in the center of the dough and then fold the bottom third of the dough over to cover half of the butter. Next fold the top third of dough over to cover the remaining half of the butter.

6 Rotate the dough by a quarter turn and roll out slightly. Fold the short ends over to meet in the middle. Wrap in plastic wrap and chill in the fridge for 30 minutes.

7 Repeat this rolling and folding process twice and then wrap and chill for at least 2 hours or, better still, overnight.

8 Line 2 baking sheets with baking parchment.

9 On a lightly floured surface, roll out the dough to a large rectangle, about 24 x 12 in (60 x 30cm) and trim the edges. Cut the dough into long triangles and gently stretch the corners at the base of each triangle to make it wider.

10 Starting at the wide base, gently roll up each triangle, working your way down to the point; tuck the point underneath. Bend the ends inward and place on the prepared baking sheets, leaving a little space between them.

11 Cover the baking sheets with plastic wrap and set aside for 2 hours at room temperature until the croissants double in size. Preheat the oven to 400°F/200°C.

12 Brush the croissants generously with beaten egg and then bake for 15–20 minutes until well risen and crisp. Cool on a wire rack before serving.

Matcha pancakes with maple syrup

Two of our favorite things—matcha and pancakes. Actually, matcha *in* pancakes. For a savory brunch, serve the pancakes with crispy bacon strips or grilled tomatoes and mushrooms.

SERVES 4

1¼ cups (150g) self-rising flour
1 tbsp matcha powder
2 tbsp superfine sugar
2 eggs
½ cup (125ml) milk or buttermilk
2 tbsp butter, melted
sunflower or olive oil, for frying
maple syrup, to serve
blueberries for garnish

1 Preheat the oven on a very low setting—no more than 300°F/150°C.

2 Sift the flour into a large bowl and mix in the matcha powder and sugar. Make a well in the center.

3 In another bowl, whisk the eggs and then beat in the milk or buttermilk until well combined. Stir in the melted butter and pour into the well in the flour mixture. Whisk together until you have a smooth batter.

4 Place a large skillet over medium heat and add a little oil. When it's hot, drop large spoonfuls of batter into the skillet, leaving plenty of space between the pancakes. Cook for 1–2 minutes until golden underneath, then flip the pancakes over and cook the other side.

5 Remove to a plate and keep warm in the oven while you cook the remaining pancakes in the same way.

6 Divide the pancakes between four warm serving plates and serve immediately with maple syrup and a scattering of blueberries.

VARIATIONS
• Serve the pancakes with sliced banana or fresh raspberries or strawberries.
• Try adding a good pinch of cinnamon to the pancake mixture for a more subtle, spicy flavor.

Matcha eggs Florentine

This isn't the most obvious culinary combination, but trust us: it works. It looks impressive, too! For Matcha eggs Benedict, simply omit the spinach and top the eggs and Hollandaise sauce with thin strips of crispy back bacon.

SERVES 2

7 oz (200g) baby spinach leaves
2 tsp white wine vinegar
4 eggs
2 English muffins, lightly toasted

FOR THE MATCHA HOLLANDAISE SAUCE
1 stick (125g) butter, diced
2 egg yolks
½ tbsp cold water
½ tbsp lemon juice
1 tsp matcha powder
salt and freshly ground
    black pepper to taste

1 To make the hollandaise sauce: put the butter, egg yolks, and water in a small saucepan over low heat. Heat very gently, whisking continuously (use an electric one to make it easier), as the butter melts and the sauce starts to thicken. Turn up the heat a touch and keep on whisking until the sauce thickens enough to coat the back of a spoon. Gently stir in the lemon juice, matcha powder, and seasoning to taste.

2 Remove the saucepan from the heat and then cover with a lid to keep warm.

3 Put the spinach in another saucepan, cover with a lid, and place over very low heat for 2 minutes, until the spinach wilts and turns bright green. Drain in a colander and press down with a saucer to squeeze out all the liquid.

4 Heat a large saucepan of water until it's just simmering and add the wine vinegar. Carefully break the eggs into the saucepan and poach in the gently simmering water for about 4 minutes. When the whites are set and the yolks are still runny, remove with a slotted spoon and drain on paper towels.

5 Place 2 toasted muffin halves on each serving plate and divide the spinach between them. Top each one with a poached egg and pour the hollandaise over the top. Serve immediately.

VARIATIONS
• If you're in a hurry, top the eggs with store-bought Hollandaise sauce and sprinkle with a pinch of vivid green matcha sea salt made by grinding together equal parts matcha powder and coarse sea salt crystals in a pestle and mortar.
• Substitute thinly sliced smoked salmon or tuna salad for the spinach.

Snacks

Chia seed and matcha power pots

SUPER-HEALTHY

You need to make these the night before you want to enjoy them. It's a little extra effort, but well worth doing because, as Aidan and Glen put it, these are "a real humdinger of a snack, packed with healthy fats and protein from nuts and seeds. Designed to keep hunger at bay, these power pots provide slow-burn fuel to see you comfortably through the longest of mornings or afternoons."

SERVES 4

8 tbsp chia seeds
2 cups (500ml) unsweetened
   almond milk
2 tsp matcha powder
1 tbsp runny honey or date syrup
2 ripe peaches, pitted and diced
4 tbsp Greek yogurt
1½ cups (150g) fresh blueberries
4 tbsp chopped nuts (almonds,
   hazelnuts, or pistachios)

1 Put the chia seeds and almond milk in a bowl and stir together.

2 In another bowl, blend the matcha powder and honey or date syrup until evenly mixed, then stir into the chia mixture with the diced peaches.

3 Divide the mixture between four bowls, glass pots, or screwtop jam jars and cover with plastic wrap or the screwtop lids.

4 Chill in the fridge overnight or until all the liquid absorbs and the mixture has a jelly-like texture.

5 The following day, top each pot with a spoonful of yogurt and then sprinkle with the blueberries and chopped nuts.

VARIATIONS
• Experiment with different fruit, depending on what's in season. Try diced apple or pear, strawberries, raspberries, cherries, or plums.
• Instead of fresh fruit, top with some fruit compote before swirling in the yogurt.
• Spoon a layer of mango purée into the bottom of each pot before adding the chia mixture for a colorful layered effect.

Matcha pretzels

Matcha works really well with soft, sweet breads and pretzels, and we love this pretzel recipe with its distinctive "sweet and salty" taste.

MAKES 10–12 PRETZELS

4½ cups (450g) strong white bread flour, plus extra for dusting
¼ oz (7g) instant yeast
1 tsp salt
1 tbsp soft brown sugar
3 tbsp baking soda
1 tbsp matcha powder
½ cup (125ml) warm water
½ cup (125ml) milk
2 tbsp butter, room temperature
1 egg, beaten
sea salt crystals and toasted sesame seeds

1 Put the flour, yeast, salt, sugar, and 1 tablespoon of the baking soda in a large mixing bowl and mix together. Make a well in the center.

2 Whisk the matcha powder into the warm water until it's smooth and free of lumps. Pour into the flour mixture with the milk and add the softened butter. Mix together until you have a soft, smooth dough.

3 Turn the dough out onto a lightly floured surface and knead well for 5–10 minutes until it becomes elastic, silky in texture, and doesn't stick to your fingers.

4 Place the dough in a lightly oiled bowl, then cover and set aside at room temperature for 1–2 hours until it has doubled in size.

5 Knock the dough back and knead briefly, then cut it into 10–12 equal pieces. Using your hands, stretch each piece out and roll into a sausage shape with the ends slightly slimmer than the middle. Cross the ends over each other and then fold them up and over into the center of the loop to make a classic pretzel shape (see opposite). Leave them for 30 minutes to rise a little.

6 Preheat the oven to 400°F/200°C. Line 2 baking sheets with baking parchment.

7 Bring a large saucepan of water to a boil and add the remaining baking soda. Add the pretzels, a few at a time, and boil for 20 seconds. Remove with a slotted spoon and place on the baking sheets. Brush with beaten egg and then sprinkle with sea salt and sesame seeds.

8 Bake for 12–15 minutes until golden brown and firm. Allow to cool and store in an airtight container.

Matcha pistachio protein balls

"These are a superb pick-me-up for anyone keeping active. Add your favorite dried fruits, such as chopped dates, apricots, or figs or even some raw cacao."

MAKES 12 BALLS

½ cup (75g) cashews
½ cup (40g) desiccated coconut
1 tbsp chia seeds
2 tsp matcha powder, plus extra
   for rolling
2 tbsp coconut flour
¼ cup (30g) protein powder
2 tbsp coconut oil
4 tbsp runny honey or date syrup
3–4 tbsp water
¼ cup (30g) finely chopped
   pistachio nuts

1 In a food processor or blender, pulse the cashews, coconut, chia seeds, matcha powder, coconut flour, and protein powder.

2 Melt the coconut oil in a small saucepan over low heat and add to the blended mixture with the honey and the water. Pulse briefly until you have a dough. Add a little more water if it's too dry—you want it to stick together.

3 Divide the mixture into 12 equal portions and, using your hands, roll each one into a ball.

4 Roll the balls in the pistachios and some matcha powder, then chill in the fridge until cool and firm. You can store them in an airtight container.

Raw sticky date and matcha bars

"These bars are proof that guiltless pleasure does exist! Medjool dates are a fantastic sweet treat that actually improve health and blood sugar levels."

MAKES 8–10 BARS

*2 tbsp coconut oil, plus extra
    for greasing*
*1 cup (175g) medjool dates,
    pitted*
½ cup (75g) almonds
½ cup (30g) flax seeds
1 tbsp matcha powder
1 tsp vanilla extract
1 cup (75g) rolled oats
*coconut flakes and matcha
    powder for garnish*

1 Lightly grease a small square or rectangular pan or baking dish with a little coconut oil and then line with baking parchment. Melt the coconut oil in a small saucepan over low heat.

2 Pulse the dates, almonds, matcha powder, flax seeds, vanilla extract, and melted coconut oil to a puree in a food processor. Stir in the oats. If the mixture is too loose and sticky, add more oats.

3 Spoon the mixture into the lined pan, pushing it into the corners and pressing it down evenly. Sprinkle with coconut flakes and matcha and level the top, pressing down with a spatula or spoon.

4 Chill in the fridge overnight to set. Cut into bars and store in an airtight container in the fridge.

Matcha banana bread

Packed with slow-releasing energy and potassium from the bananas, this is so yummy that you have to make it all the time.

1 cup (200g) all-purpose flour
1 tsp baking soda
1 tsp matcha powder
½ tsp salt
1 stick (125g) salted butter
1 cup (200g) light brown sugar
2 eggs
3-4 ripe bananas
2 tbsp milk
2 tbsp runny yogurt
1 tsp vanilla extract
2 oz (50g) white chocolate chips

1 Preheat the oven to 350°F/180°C. Grease a 9 x 4¾ inch (23 x 12cm) loaf tin and line with baking parchment.

2 Sift the flour, baking soda, matcha powder, and salt into a bowl and set aside.

3 Melt the butter, then, using an electric whisk, whisk the butter with the brown sugar in a large bowl until pale and fluffy. Add the eggs, one at a time, and beat well.

4 Mash the bananas, then add to the butter and sugar mix. Mix well, then stir in the milk, yogurt, and vanilla extract. Gently mix in the dry ingredients and lastly add the chocolate chips, mixing well.

5 Pour into the prepared loaf tin and bake for 35–45 minutes or until a toothpick inserted into the center comes out clean and the loaf springs back to the touch. Leave to cool for 10–15 minutes and then enjoy!

Matcha marshmallows

These fun green marshmallows are great served hot with chocolate or raspberry sauce. For an extra-green hit, add a little matcha to the confectioner's sugar and cornstarch mix.

MAKES ABOUT 36 MARSHMALLOWS

2 cups (450g) granulated sugar
1 tbsp liquid glucose or corn syrup
1½ cups (350ml) water
2 egg whites
1 tbsp matcha powder
9 sheets leaf gelatine
few drops of vanilla extract
6 tbsp confectioner's sugar
3 tbsp cornstarch

1 Put the granulated sugar, glucose or corn syrup, and 1 cup (200ml) water in a saucepan. Stir over low-medium heat to dissolve the sugar and then bring to a boil.

2 When the temperature of the sugar syrup reaches 260°F/127°C on a candy thermometer, remove the saucepan from the heat. Take care as it will be extremely hot.

3 In a large, dry bowl, beat the egg whites until they form stiff peaks. Set aside.

4 Mix the matcha powder with 2 tablespoons of the remaining water in a bowl and stir well until smooth with no lumps. Soak the gelatine in the remaining water for about 10 minutes until softened.

5 Carefully stir the matcha mixture, gelatine, and soaking liquid into the hot sugar syrup and transfer to a pitcher.

6 Gradually pour the matcha syrup onto the egg whites in a thin stream, beating all the time until really shiny. Add the vanilla and continue whisking on high speed for 8–10 minutes until the mixture holds its shape. This is best done in a food mixer, but you can use an electric whisk.

7 Lightly oil an 8 x 8in (20 x 20cm) cake pan and line with baking parchment. Combine the confectioner's sugar and cornstarch and sift some over the baking parchment.

8 Transfer the marshmallow mixture to the pan. Use wet hands or a damp step-palette knife to press down and level the top. Dust with a little more of the sugar mixture. Chill in the refrigerator for 1–2 hours until set.

9 Carefully turn out the marshmallow onto a work surface dusted with the remaining confectioner's sugar and cornstarch. Cut into squares and roll them in the sugar mixture until thoroughly coated. Store in an airtight container in a cool, dry place.

10 To serve, push the marshmallows onto thin wooden skewers and cook on a griddle or under a hot broiler for 1–2 minutes until toasted.

Raw matcha coconut fudge bites

If you love chocolate, why not add some cocoa powder to the mix, or even some cacao nibs. Alternatively, dust the fudge squares with unsweetened cocoa powder.

**MAKES ABOUT 20
BITE-SIZED SQUARES**

6 tbsp coconut oil
*2 cups (175g) unsweetened
    desiccated coconut, plus
    extra for garnish*
4–5 tbsp agave syrup
few drops of vanilla extract
pinch of fine sea salt
2 tsp matcha powder

1 Line a small square brownie pan with baking parchment.

2 Melt the coconut oil in a small saucepan over low heat.

3 Put the desiccated coconut, most of the syrup, vanilla, sea salt, and matcha powder in a food processor or blender and pulse with the melted coconut oil until well mixed and there are no clumps of matcha powder. If it's not sweet enough for your taste, add some more syrup.

4 Spoon the mixture into the lined pan and press down well to level the top. Chill in the fridge for 1–2 hours until firm.

5 Cut the fudge into squares and remove from the pan. Sprinkle with desiccated coconut and store in a sealed container in the fridge. You can also freeze it.

VARIATIONS
• Substitute maple or coconut syrup for the agave syrup.
• Experiment by using coconut butter or even almond butter instead of coconut oil.

Tip
Because coconut oil melts and becomes liquid in a warm room, you must keep the fudge in the freezer or fridge.

Main Dishes

Quinoa salad with matcha chile dressing

SUPER-HEALTHY

This is an extremely versatile summer salad. Instead of quinoa, you can use couscous or bulghur wheat or try adding cubes of salty feta or smoked tofu.

SERVES 4

1 cup (200g) quinoa
2 cups (480ml) vegetable stock
2 tbsp olive oil
1 red onion, diced
1 large ripe avocado, peeled, pitted, and diced
2 oz (60g) arugula
handful of cilantro, chopped
small bunch of chives, snipped
salt and freshly ground black pepper to taste
2 tbsp mixed pumpkin and sunflower seeds

FOR THE MATCHA CHILE DRESSING

juice of 1 lemon
½ tsp matcha powder
1 small red chile, deseeded and finely chopped
few drops of runny honey
4 tbsp olive oil

1 Rinse the quinoa under running cold water and drain. Bring the stock to a boil in a saucepan and then add the quinoa. Reduce the heat, cover the saucepan, and simmer gently for 15 minutes until the quinoa is tender and has absorbed most of the stock. When the quinoa is cooked, the "sprouts" or "tails" will pop out of the seeds.

2 Remove from the heat and leave to steam in the pan for 6–8 minutes before draining the excess liquid. Fluff the quinoa with a fork.

3 Stir in the olive oil, red onion, avocado, arugula, cilantro, and chives. Season to taste with salt and pepper.

4 To make the dressing: mix together the lemon juice and matcha powder until thoroughly amalgamated. Stir in the chile and honey, then whisk in the oil. Alternatively, shake everything together in a cruet or screwtop jar.

5 Toss the quinoa salad in the dressing until completely coated. Sprinkle with the pumpkin and sunflower seeds and serve.

VARIATIONS

• Use orange juice in the dressing and add some grated fresh ginger or crushed garlic.
• Most herbs work well, so don't worry if you don't have or like fresh cilantro or chives. Try parsley, basil, or mint.
• You can also add grilled or roasted vegetables, including beetroot, asparagus, bell peppers, zucchini, and eggplant.

Matcha poached salmon, broccoli, and chickpea salad

SUPER-HEALTHY

"This delicious salad combines salmon, which is rich in omega-3 fats, with the flavonoid-rich matcha, both of which show promise as 'brain foods,' with the potential to stave off cognitive decline."

SERVES 2

FOR THE SALMON
1 cup (200ml) water, plus 1 tbsp
    for the paste
pinch of chile flakes
½ tsp black peppercorns
½ lemon, thinly sliced
1 tsp matcha powder
¼ cup (50ml) sake or mirin
2 salmon fillets, each about
    4½ oz (125g), skin on

FOR THE SALAD
8 florets of broccoli
2 slices of lemon
4 handfuls of spinach leaves
1 can (14 oz/400g) chickpeas,
    drained and rinsed
4 scallions, chopped

FOR THE DRESSING
4 tbsp nam pla (Thai fish sauce)
½ tsp matcha powder
juice of 2 limes
2 tbsp sweet chile sauce
1 Thai bird's eye red chile,
    finely diced

TO SERVE
lemon wedges (optional)

1 Pour the cup of water into a large, deep, lidded skillet, then add the chile flakes and black peppercorns to the water. Bring the water to a boil over high heat, then reduce to low. Add the lemon slices.

2 Meanwhile, add the matcha to 1 tbsp of hot (not boiling) water in a small bowl or jug and whisk to make a paste.

3 Add the matcha paste to the simmering water and stir until mixed. Add the sake or mirin, then place the salmon in the skillet, skin-side down. Cover and leave to cook for 8 minutes, then remove from the poaching liquid and discard the liquid.

4 Meanwhile, bring some water to a boil in a steamer and steam the broccoli and lemon slices for 7 minutes, then remove from the heat.

5 To make the dressing, whisk half the nam pla in a large bowl with the matcha powder until combined. Add the rest of the dressing ingredients and mix well.

6 To make the salad, divide the spinach, chickpeas, and scallions between two serving plates, then top with the steamed broccoli, discarding the lemon slices.

7 Top the salad with the dressing, reserving a little to drizzle over the salmon. Flake the salmon, discarding the skin, and checking there are no bones, then place on top of the salad and drizzle the remaining dressing. Serve with lemon wedges if desired.

Shrimp satay salad with matcha dressing

SUPER-HEALTHY

"This is a lean and mean protein-rich salad that doesn't scrimp on plant goodness. It's light, refreshing, fruity, and crunchy, and the matcha satay dressing gives it a wonderful creaminess."

SERVES 4

FOR THE SATAY MARINADE, DRESSING, AND SHRIMP

1 tsp matcha powder
4 tsp soy sauce
2 garlic cloves, crushed
1 inch (2.5cm) piece of fresh root ginger, grated
4 tsp smooth, all-natural peanut butter (no added salt, sugar, or oil)
4 tsp hoisin sauce
juice of 1 lime
1 tsp runny honey
10½ oz (300g) raw shrimp
3 tbsp coconut milk

FOR THE SALAD

2 carrots
¼ cucumber
1 apple, grated
2 sticks celery, finely sliced widthways
4 scallions, chopped
4 oz (100g) arugula
2 tsp sesame seeds
2 tsp pumpkin seeds

1 To make the satay marinade and dressing, add the matcha to the soy sauce in a bowl or jar and whisk well. Add the garlic, ginger, peanut butter, hoisin sauce, lime juice, and honey and stir well.

2 Divide the mixture in half and use one half to marinate the shrimp. Spread the marinade over the shrimp in a large container and set aside. Reserve the other half of the mixture to make the dressing.

3 To make the salad, peel the carrot and then, using a potato peeler, peel the carrots and cucumber into long thin strips/ribbons. Mix the ribbons with the grated apple, celery, and scallions.

4 Divide the arugula between four serving plates, then top with the cucumber and apple mix. Sprinkle the sesame and pumpkin seeds over the top.

5 Finish the dressing by adding the coconut milk to the reserved dressing. Mix well and drizzle over the salad.

6 Finally, heat a wok or deep skillet until hot, add the shrimp along with their marinade, and stir-fry for 5 minutes. When cooked, add to the salad plates and serve straight away.

Steak and noodle salad with matcha dressing

SUPER-HEALTHY

Bursting with flavor from the fresh herbs, chiles, and limes, this vibrant salad works just as well with grilled chicken, jumbo shrimp, or salmon if you don't want to use steak.

SERVES 4

9 oz (250g) rice noodles
2 large carrots
½ cucumber
6 fresh lime leaves, stems and
    central veins removed
10 oz (300g) bean sprouts
1 small bunch of cilantro,
    roughly chopped
handful of mint, chopped
8 cherry tomatoes, halved
    or quartered
3 lean strip loin steaks, visible
    fat removed
pinch of sea salt
6 tbsp unsalted peanuts, toasted
    and chopped (tip below)

FOR THE MATCHA DRESSING
juice of 1 lime
2 tbsp nam pla (Thai fish sauce)
1 tsp light soy sauce
1 garlic clove, crushed
pinch of superfine sugar
1 red Thai bird's eye chile,
    deseeded and shredded
1 tsp matcha powder

1 Put the rice noodles in a bowl and cover with cold water. Leave them to soak for about 15 minutes, until softened. Drain well and set aside.

2 Peel the carrots and then, using a potato peeler, peel them into long thin strips. Cut the cucumber in half. Use a potato peeler to cut it into long strips. Roll up the lime leaves and shred them as thinly as possible.

3 Put the carrots, cucumber, lime leaves, bean sprouts, cilantro, mint, and tomatoes in a serving dish.

4 Mix all the dressing ingredients together, whisking in the matcha powder a little at a time until well combined and no clumps remain. Alternatively, shake everything vigorously in a cruet or screwtop jar.

5 Cook the steaks on a lightly oiled griddle or ridged grill pan on high heat for a couple of minutes on each side until charred on the outside but still pink inside. Slice them thickly and sprinkle with sea salt.

6 Add the rice noodles to the vegetables and toss gently in the dressing. Divide between four plates and add the steak. Sprinkle with the peanuts and serve immediately while the steak is still warm.

VARIATIONS
• Try adding a spoonful of sweet chile sauce to the dressing or drizzle some over the top.
• Arugula or watercress are healthy additions and add a peppery flavor. Also try baby spinach leaves or finely shredded kale.

 Tip
To toast the peanuts, put them in a single layer in a non-stick skillet over medium heat. Toss them in the hot skillet for 2–3 minutes, taking care not to let them burn, until golden brown all over. Remove immediately.

Matcha gnocchi with sage and orange sauce

This recipe is perfect for a chilly fall evening. Add a pinch of grated nutmeg to the flour and matcha when making the gnocchi for a more distinctive, subtly spicy flavor.

SERVES 4

1 lb 2 oz (500g) Yukon Gold
    potatoes, washed and dried
1½ cups (175g) all-purpose flour,
    plus extra for dusting
pinch of salt
1 tbsp matcha powder
1 egg, beaten
grated Parmesan, to sprinkle
snipped chives, to sprinkle

FOR THE SAGE AND ORANGE SAUCE
½ cup (100g) butter
6 sage leaves
juice of 1 large orange
salt and freshly ground
    black pepper to taste

1 Preheat the oven to 375°F/190°C.

2 To make the gnocchi: Prick the potatoes all over with a fork and place on a baking sheet. Bake in the oven for about 1 hour, until cooked and tender. Remove from the oven and let cool.

3 When the potatoes are cool enough to handle, remove the skins.

4 On a clean work surface, sprinkle about two-thirds of the flour plus the salt and matcha powder. Push the potatoes through a fine sieve or a potato ricer and add to the flour. Make a well in the center and add the beaten egg. Mix everything together with your hands, gradually adding more flour as and when needed. You should end up with a soft dough. Do not over-mix.

5 Roll out or flatten the dough into a square, about ½ in (1.25cm) thick, on a floured work surface. Cut it into ½ in (1.25cm) wide strips and roll each one into a long cylindrical sausage shape. Next, cut each sausage into smaller pieces, dust lightly with flour, and then press each one lightly with the tines of a fork to leave indentations.

6 To make the sauce: Melt the butter over low heat in a large skillet. Add the whole sage leaves and heat through for 1 minute, just long enough to allow the flavor to permeate the sauce. Stir in the orange juice and season to taste with salt and pepper. Remove and discard the sage leaves.

7 Bring a large saucepan of water to a boil, then reduce the heat to a simmer. Add the gnocchi and give them a gentle stir. When they all rise to the surface and float, count to 10 and then remove with a slotted spoon.

8 Add the gnocchi to the hot sauce and divide between four serving plates. Sprinkle with Parmesan and chives and serve immediately.

Shiitake, bok choy, and matcha teriyaki stir-fry

SUPER HEALTHY

Here we've combined two treasured Japanese foods in a dish that indulges your immune system. "Shiitake is a 'medicinal mushroom' and is studied extensively for its potent immune—and wellness—enhancing effects." With the matcha addition, you can't go wrong!

SERVES 2

FOR THE TERIYAKI SAUCE
1 tbsp runny honey
2 tbsp light soy sauce
2 tbsp water
2 tbsp sesame oil
2 tbsp grated fresh root ginger
1 garlic clove, chopped
1 tsp matcha powder

FOR THE STIR-FRY
1 tbsp coconut oil
1½ inch (4cm) piece of fresh root ginger, finely chopped
2 garlic cloves
½ onion, finely chopped
2 scallions, finely chopped
4½ oz (125g) shiitake mushrooms
3 bulbs bok choy, chopped

1 cup (200g) steamed brown rice, to serve

1 Make the teriyaki sauce by combining all the ingredients for the sauce, stirring well so there are no lumps of matcha powder.

2 Place a large wok or deep skillet over medium-high heat. Add the coconut oil, and when the pan is hot, stir-fry the ginger and garlic until soft, about 3 minutes. Add the onion and stir-fry for 2–3 minutes, then add the scallions and cook for another minute.

3 Add the mushrooms and cook for 1 minute, then add the teriyaki sauce and stir-fry for about 5 minutes.

4 Finally add the bok choy and toss in the hot wok for about 2 minutes, then remove from the heat, divide between two bowls, and serve with steamed brown rice.

Wasabi tuna with matcha green beans

SUPER-HEALTHY

Packed with taste, this Japanese-influenced dish works equally well with fresh salmon instead of tuna and goes great with either rice noodles or rice.

SERVES 4

14 oz (400g) fresh tuna
2 tbsp soy sauce
1 tsp grated or finely diced fresh root ginger
2 tsp wasabi paste
1 tsp sesame oil, plus extra for brushing
9 oz (250g) thin green beans, trimmed
sesame seeds, for sprinkling
boiled or steamed rice, to serve

FOR THE MATCHA DRESSING
1 tbsp rice wine vinegar
1 tsp matcha powder
3 tbsp sesame oil
1 tbsp teriyaki sauce

1 Cut the tuna into 1 in (2.5cm) chunks and place in a bowl with 1 tbsp of the soy sauce. Turn the tuna pieces gently until they are coated with the sauce and then push them onto 4 wooden skewers that have soaked in warm water (tip below).

2 Mix the remaining soy sauce with the ginger, wasabi paste, and sesame oil.

3 To make the matcha dressing: Put the vinegar in a small bowl and stir or whisk in the matcha powder until thoroughly mixed. Whisk in the sesame oil and teriyaki sauce.

4 Steam the green beans until they are al dente or cook them in a saucepan of boiling water for about 5–7 minutes. Drain well and toss them immediately in the matcha dressing.

5 Heat a griddle pan over medium-high heat and brush with a little oil. Place the tuna skewers on the hot griddle and cook for 2 minutes each side until seared all over. Sprinkle with the wasabi mixture and cook for 1 minute. The tuna should be slightly pink on the inside and seared outside. If you like it more well done, cook for another minute.

6 Serve the tuna skewers, sprinkled with sesame seeds, on a bed of the matcha green beans.

VARIATIONS
• Cook the tuna steaks on the griddle instead of making them into kebabs, but note that they will take longer to cook as steaks.
• Vary the green vegetables—try steamed bok choy or Chinese cabbage.

 Tip
Soaking the wooden or bamboo skewers in warm water for at least 20 minutes before use will prevent them from burning.

Matcha Thai green curry with jumbo shrimp

SUPER HEALTHY

This is our take on the classic Thai green curry. It's delightfully creamy and coconuty, with a subtle taste of matcha green tea.

SERVES 4

14 oz (400g) rice noodles
oil, for grilling
1 tbsp coconut oil
2 garlic cloves, crushed
2 in (5cm) piece of fresh root
    ginger, peeled and diced
1 lemongrass stalk, peeled and
    diced
1 bunch scallions, thinly sliced
1 lb (450g) bok choy, shredded
2 tsp matcha powder
1¼ cups (300ml) chicken stock,
    warmed
2½ cups (600ml) reduced-fat
    coconut milk
grated zest and juice of 1 lime
2 tsp nam pla (Thai fish sauce)
1 tbsp Thai green curry paste
1 tbsp coconut palm sugar
17½ oz (500g) raw jumbo shrimp
    (shell on)
large handful of Thai basil,
    chopped
salt and freshly ground black
    pepper to taste
shredded scallions for garnish
lime wedges for garnish

1 Cook the rice noodles according to the instructions on the packet. Preheat a lightly oiled griddle pan until hot.

2 Heat the coconut oil in a large saucepan over a medium heat. Add the garlic, ginger, lemongrass, scallions, and bok choy and cook, stirring once or twice, for 3 minutes.

3 Mix the matcha powder with a little of the warm stock, stirring well, and then add to the vegetables in the saucepan with the remaining stock and the coconut milk.

4 Add the lime zest and juice, nam pla, Thai green curry paste, and palm sugar and heat gently until piping hot.

5 Meanwhile, cook the shrimp on the hot griddle pan for about 2 minutes on each side, leaving the shells on at least the tails. The shrimp should turn pink and be juicy. Don't overcook them or they will become tough.

6 Stir the chopped Thai basil and drained rice noodles into the curry. Season to taste with salt and pepper.

7 Ladle the curry into four bowls and arrange the grilled shrimp and shredded scallions on top. Garnish with lime wedges and serve immediately.

VARIATIONS
• You can add a little heat to the broth by cooking a diced chile with the garlic and ginger mixture in step 2 above. Or sprinkle the curry with some shredded chile as a garnish.
• Instead of shrimp, try grilled chicken breasts.

Chicken, turmeric, matcha, and pepper one-pot meal

SUPER HEALTHY

"This spicy number contains powerful natural anti-inflammatory plant compounds, most notably the turmeric. But it's the synergy of the ingredients that really amplifies these benefits. The EGCG from the matcha enhances turmeric's effects in the body, while the piperine from the black pepper and the presence of fats increase turmeric's absorption."

SERVES 4

1 chicken stock cube
2½ cups (500g) green lentils
1 lb 2 oz (500g) skinless chicken thighs or a mixture of thighs and legs
salt
2 tbsp freshly ground black pepper
1 tbsp coconut oil
1 onion, finely chopped
1 inch (2.5cm) piece of fresh root ginger, finely chopped
2 garlic cloves, finely chopped or crushed
juice of ½ lemon
2 tsp turmeric
2 tsp matcha powder
1 cup (240ml) water, plus 2 tbsp warm water
9 oz (250g) spinach leaves
flatbread, to serve

1 First prepare the lentils. Bring a saucepan of water to a boil and add the stock cube. Add the lentils and cook, uncovered, for 20 minutes. Drain and set aside.

2 Place the chicken pieces in a large bowl and season well with salt. Then add lots of black pepper so it completely coats the chicken.

3 Over medium heat, in a large casserole or other lidded oven-proof dish, heat the coconut oil and then gently fry the onion, ginger, and garlic. Season with a little salt and pepper.

4 Once the onion, ginger, and garlic are soft, add the peppered chicken to the casserole dish and fry for 3–4 minutes until browned. The pepper should give the chicken a good, firm coating. Add the lemon juice, then the turmeric, and mix well.

5 Next add the matcha to a jar or bowl, add 2 tbsp of warm water, and whisk well. Add the rest of the measured water to the matcha and then add the matcha to the oven-proof dish. Cover the dish and cook over low heat for 25 minutes, stirring occasionally so it doesn't stick.

6 Add the spinach and cooked lentils to the chicken curry, stir in well, and cook for 3 more minutes. Serve with flatbread.

Mexican chicken with matcha guacamole

SUPER-HEALTHY

This is a great midweek dinner to share with friends especially since our nutritionists, Aidan and Glen, encourage regularly eating hot, spicy food for the health benefits of chiles.

SERVES 4

grated zest and juice of 2 limes
1 tsp chile flakes or diced
    red chile
2 garlic cloves, crushed
1 tbsp olive or peanut oil
salt and freshly ground black
    pepper to taste
4 chicken breasts, skinned and
    boned
1 bunch of scallions, trimmed
warmed tortillas, to serve

FOR THE MATCHA GUACAMOLE

1 fresh green chile, diced
½ red onion, diced
1 garlic clove, crushed
¼ tsp sea salt
2 ripe avocados
juice of 1 lime
1 small bunch of cilantro,
    chopped
1 tsp matcha powder
1 ripe tomato, deseeded
    and diced
freshly ground black pepper

1 In a bowl, mix together the lime zest and juice, chile, garlic, and oil for the marinade. Add salt and pepper to taste.

2 Slash each chicken breast 3 or 4 times with a sharp knife and add to the marinade, turning until the chicken is completely coated. Set aside while you make the guacamole.

3 Crush the chile, red onion, garlic, and salt in a pestle and mortar. Cut the avocados in half and remove the pits. Scoop out the flesh and mash roughly with a fork—it shouldn't be too smooth. Stir in the lime juice. Add the cilantro, crushed red onion mixture, matcha powder, and diced tomato. Mix everything together and add a grinding of black pepper.

4 Cook the chicken on an oiled griddle pan or under a preheated broiler for 8–10 minutes on each side until sticky and golden brown on the outside and cooked through inside. Remove and keep warm.

5 Add the scallions to the hot griddle and cook for 1–2 minutes on each side until slightly seared and just tender.

6 Cut the hot chicken into slices and serve immediately with the scallions, matcha guacamole, and warmed tortillas.

VARIATIONS

• Make it a burrito. Divide the chicken between the tortillas and add some guacamole, a spoonful of hot salsa, some sour cream or plain Greek yogurt, and griddled bell peppers. Roll up and enjoy.
• Instead of scallions, cook some sliced red, green, and yellow bell peppers and red onions on the griddle to serve with the chicken.

Stir-fried pork and matcha soba noodles

SUPER-HEALTHY

Our nutritionists love soba noodles, made from buckwheat, a nutritious, high-protein, gluten-free, versatile "pseudo-grain." They're full of minerals and fiber and taste great, so make them a pantry staple. For a more zingy flavor, include some grated lime zest and juice; for a bit of crunch, add cashew nuts.

SERVES 4

10 oz (300g) matcha soba
    noodles
1 tbsp sesame oil
3 tbsp coconut oil
1 tbsp freshly grated ginger
1 red chile, deseeded and diced
1 garlic clove, crushed
1 bunch of scallions, sliced
    diagonally
1 red bell pepper, deseeded and
    thinly sliced
10 oz (300g) bok choy, shredded
2 tbsp light soy sauce
2 tsp nam pla (Thai fish sauce)
4 tbsp chicken or vegetable stock
1 tsp superfine sugar
12 oz (350g) lean pork tenderloin,
    thinly sliced
freshly ground peppercorns
    (black or Szechuan)
roughly chopped cilantro
    for garnish

1 Cook the noodles in a saucepan of salted boiling water according to the packet instructions. They should be *al dente*. Drain well.

2 Meanwhile, place a large wok or deep skillet over medium-high heat. Add the sesame oil and 2 tbsp of the coconut oil. When the pan is really hot, stir-fry the ginger, chile, and garlic for 1 minute.

3 Add the scallions, red bell pepper, and bok choy and toss in the hot wok until the bok choy starts to wilt.

4 Stir in the drained noodles, soy sauce, nam pla, stock, and sugar. Stir-fry for 2 minutes.

5 Fry the pork briskly in the remaining coconut oil in a separate skillet over high heat for 4–5 minutes, until golden brown on both sides and thoroughly cooked. Grind plenty of pepper over the top.

6 Divide the stir-fried noodle mixture between four serving plates and top with the pork. Sprinkle with cilantro and serve immediately.

VARIATION
• Use different vegetables: sliced shiitake and oyster mushrooms, bean sprouts, shredded kale, or broccoli. All work well.

Note

If you fancy making your own matcha noodles, follow a basic recipe for fresh egg pasta, adding 1 tbsp matcha powder per 10 oz (300g) Tipo 00 or semolina flour. We recommend making the pasta in a food processor and using a pasta machine to roll and cut it into strips.

Cakes and Cookies

Chocolate layer cake with matcha frosting

Wow, wow, wow! This is a truly impressive, truly indulgent celebration cake. Enjoy it with a Matcha latte (page 58) or a Matcha mint fizz (page 66).

MAKES ONE 8 IN/20CM CAKE

1 cup (225g) butter
1 cup (225g) superfine sugar
4 eggs
1½ cups (175g) self-rising flour
½ cup (60g) cocoa powder
½ tsp baking powder
chocolate cake decorations (optional)

FOR THE MATCHA BUTTERCREAM FROSTING

1 tbsp matcha powder
2 tbsp milk
1 cup (225g) unsalted butter, room temperature
4 cups (450g) confectioner's sugar

1 Preheat the oven to 375°F/190°C. Lightly butter two 8 in (20cm) cake pans and line the bases with baking parchment.

2 Cream the butter and sugar in a food mixer or processor until light and fluffy. Beat in the eggs, one at a time, adding a little flour with each one to prevent the mixture from curdling.

3 Sift the remaining flour with the cocoa powder and baking powder and add to the mixture on a slow speed until thoroughly blended. If it seems too thick, thin it with a little milk.

4 Divide the mixture between the two lined cake pans and lightly smooth the top. Bake for 20–25 minutes until well risen and the sponge is starting to come away from the sides of the pans. When you press it gently, it should spring back.

5 Leave to cool for 10 minutes before turning out onto a wire rack. When at room temperature remove the lining paper.

6 To make the matcha buttercream frosting: Blend the matcha powder and milk in a small bowl until you have a smooth paste. In a food mixer or processor or with an electric whisk, beat the butter until soft and then gradually beat in the confectioner's sugar with the matcha paste until the frosting is thick and smooth.

7 Cut each cake in half horizontally with a long-bladed knife. Spread the frosting over three of the sponges and sandwich them together. Top with the remaining sponge layer and cover with the rest of the frosting, smoothing it with a step-palette knife.

8 Decorate the cake with chocolate shards or curls if you like.

VARIATION
• Add some chocolate chips to the cake mixture or 2 tbsp espresso.

Matcha Swiss roll

The combination of matcha with this lemony filling is gorgeous. This lovely dessert goes well with fresh strawberries or raspberries. Also try orange marmalade rather than lemon curd.

SERVES 8

oil, for greasing
½ cup (125g) superfine sugar,
*   plus extra for dusting*
1 cup (125g) all-purpose flour,
*   plus extra for dusting*
3 large eggs
1 tbsp matcha powder
1 tbsp tepid water

FOR THE FILLING
1¼ cups (300ml) heavy cream
4 tbsp lemon curd

1 Preheat the oven to 400°F/200°C. Lightly brush a 13 x 9 in (33 x 23cm) baking sheet with oil and then line with baking parchment. Brush the paper with oil and then lightly dust with superfine sugar and flour.

2 Put the eggs and sugar in a large mixing bowl and beat with an electric whisk until the mixture is pale and thick (about three times the original volume) and leaves a trail when you lift the whisk into the air. Be patient and don't take shortcuts. This step is key! You may have to keep whisking for 10 full minutes to get to this stage.

3 Sift the flour into a clean bowl and gently stir in the matcha powder until thoroughly mixed. Tip half into the cake mixture and mix in gently but thoroughly with a metal spoon in a figure-eight movement. Repeat with the remaining flour. Fold in the water.

4 Pour the mixture onto the prepared baking sheet and spread it out evenly into the corners. Bake for 10–12 minutes until risen and firm to the touch.

5 Place a clean damp kitchen towel on the work surface and a large sheet of baking parchment on top of that. Dust the baking parchment with sugar.

6 Loosen the warm sponge by running a knife around the edge and gently invert it onto the sugar-dusted baking parchment. Carefully peel away the top baking parchment and neatly trim the edges of the sponge. Cover with another sheet of baking parchment and roll it up gently from one of the short ends, using the baking parchment and kitchen towel underneath to help you. Don't worry if it cracks a little—just roll it slowly and make sure the towel underneath is damp to help prevent cracking.

7 To make the filling, whip the cream in a bowl until thick. Gently swirl in the lemon curd to create a marbled effect.

8 When the sponge is room temperature, gently unroll it and spread the filling, leaving a small border around the edge. Gently and slowly roll up the cake (still prone to cracking) and place it, seam-side down, on a plate. Dust with sugar and serve in slices.

Coconut and matcha cupcakes

Coconut and matcha is one of our favorite combinations. These cupcakes are just divine—light and fluffy with delicious frosting.

MAKES 12 CUPCAKES

½ stick (60g) butter
¾ cup (175g) superfine sugar
1 large egg
1 cup (125g) all-purpose flour
1 tsp baking powder
¼ tsp baking soda
pinch of salt
1 tbsp matcha powder
½ cup (120ml) coconut milk
toasted coconut flakes for
*   garnish*

FOR THE FROSTING
2 cups (250g) confectioner's
*   sugar*
5 tbsp unsalted butter
1 tbsp matcha powder
2 tbsp coconut cream

1 Preheat the oven to 350°F/180°C. Line a 12-hole muffin tin with cupcake liners.

2 In a food mixer or processor, beat the butter and sugar until the mixture is light and fluffy. Add the egg and beat well.

3 Sift the flour, baking powder, baking soda, salt, and matcha powder into a bowl.

4 Gradually add the dry ingredients to the cake mixture, beating until well mixed. Beat in the coconut milk, a little at a time.

5 Divide the cake mixture between the cupcake liners and bake for about 15–20 minutes, until the cakes are well risen and spring back when you press them lightly with a finger. Cool on a wire rack.

6 Meanwhile, to make the coconut matcha frosting: Beat together the confectioner's sugar, butter, and matcha powder in a food mixer or processor until well blended and creamy. On a slow speed, add the coconut cream and then beat on a higher speed until the frosting is really fluffy. This may take a few minutes. Alternatively, you can make this in a large bowl with an electric whisk.

7 When the cakes have cooled completely, top them with the frosting and sprinkle with coconut flakes. They will stay fresh for 3 days if stored in an airtight container.

VARIATIONS
• Omit the matcha powder from the frosting and lightly sprinkle a little over the tops of the cupcakes instead of coconut flakes.
• Add the grated zest and juice of 1 lime to the cupcake mixture and sprinkle some finely shredded lime zest over the frosting.

Matcha blondies

These heavenly matcha blondies are a Friday afternoon treat in the teapigs' office. We hope you love them as much as we do!

MAKES ABOUT 12 BLONDIES

1 cup (200g) butter
7 oz (200g) white chocolate, chopped
1 cup (250g) soft brown sugar or muscovado sugar
3 eggs
2 cups (200g) self-rising flour
pinch of salt
1 tsp vanilla extract
3 tsp matcha powder, plus extra for dusting
confectioner's sugar for dusting

1 Preheat the oven to 350°F/180°C. Line the base of a 10 x 10 in (25 x 25cm) brownie pan with baking parchment.

2 Melt the butter in a saucepan and cook it very gently over a low heat for about 5 minutes until it turns golden.

3 Take the saucepan off the heat, add half the white chocolate, and stir until smooth. Leave to cool.

4 In a large bowl, beat the sugar and eggs together until pale and fluffy. Add the flour, salt, vanilla, matcha powder, and the cooled chocolate-butter mix and fold it all in until it's evenly mixed.

5 Pour the mixture into the pan then scatter the rest of the white chocolate over the top of the mix. Bake for 40 minutes or until completely risen. Leave to cool, then dust with a little matcha powder and confectioner's sugar.

Matcha ring doughnuts

These doughnuts are great fun to make. Once you've got the hang of the recipe, experiment with different spices, such as nutmeg or cinnamon.

MAKES ABOUT 12 DOUGHNUTS

2½ cups (300g) all-purpose flour, plus extra for dusting
2 tsp matcha powder
3 tsp baking powder
½ tsp baking soda
½ tsp salt
¼ cup (60g) granulated sugar
1 large egg
½ cup (150ml) buttermilk
2 tbsp butter, melted
vegetable oil for deep-frying

FOR THE GLAZE
2 cups (250g) confectioner's sugar
1 tbsp matcha powder
1 egg white
1 tbsp water

1 To make the matcha glaze: Sift the confectioner's sugar into a bowl and stir in the matcha powder. Add the egg white and water and whisk everything together until well combined. Set aside while you make the doughnuts.

2 Put the flour, matcha powder, baking powder, baking soda, salt, and sugar in a large bowl and mix together. Make a well in the center.

3 In a separate bowl, beat together the egg, buttermilk, and melted butter. Pour into the flour mixture and stir well until it forms a sticky dough.

4 Turn the dough out onto a floured work surface and roll it out or pat it down with your hands to a thickness of ½ in (1.25cm). Cut into rounds with a 3 in (8cm) pastry cutter. Use a smaller cutter, about 1 in (2.5cm), to make a hole in the center of each round. Roll out the leftover dough to make more doughnuts.

5 Meanwhile, pour some vegetable oil into a deep, heavy-based saucepan to a depth of 4 in (10cm) and place over medium heat. When it reaches 350°F/180°C on a candy thermometer, start frying the doughnuts.

6 Fry the doughnuts in batches, three at a time, for about 3 minutes until golden, turning them halfway through. Remove and drain on paper towels.

7 Dip the warm doughnuts in the matcha glaze and eat them while they're fresh and still warm.

VARIATION
• Instead of a glaze, try dipping the warm doughnuts in a sifted and combined mixture of confectioner's sugar and matcha powder. You will need 1 tbsp matcha powder and 1 cup (125g) confectioner's sugar.

Matcha macarons

These macarons are truly delicious because matcha works so well with almonds. These delicate and sweet little treats look very cool and amazingly green!

**MAKES ABOUT
30 MACARONS**

1½ cups (175g) confectioner's
    sugar
1 cup (175g) ground almonds
1 tsp matcha powder
4 egg whites, divided in half
¾ cup (175g) granulated sugar
¼ cup (50ml) water
a few drops green food coloring
    (optional)

**FOR THE MATCHA
BUTTERCREAM**
½ cup (125g) unsalted butter
1 cup (125g) confectioner's sugar
1 tbsp matcha powder
1 tbsp milk

1 Put the confectioner's sugar, ground almonds, and matcha powder in a food processor and pulse until well mixed and finely ground. Sift into a large mixing bowl and if any particles remain in the sieve, pulse and sift them again.

2 Add 2 egg whites and mix with a wooden spoon until you have a thick paste.

3 Put the remaining 2 egg whites in a heatproof bowl. Set aside while you make the sugar syrup.

4 To make the sugar syrup, put the granulated sugar and water in a small saucepan over medium-high heat. Stir to dissolve the sugar and bring to a boil. Cook the syrup until it reaches 225°F/110°C on a candy thermometer.

5 Immediately start beating the egg whites with an electric whisk on the high setting. As soon as the syrup reaches 239°F/118°C remove from the heat and pour it in a thin stream into the egg whites, whisking continuously on high speed until the meringue looks glossy with stiff peaks and cools slightly.

6 Gently fold half of the meringue into the matcha almond mixture with a spatula, taking care not to over-mix it. Fold in the remaining meringue and 2–3 drops of food coloring (optional). Add this very carefully, one drop at a time, until the mixture turns pale green. Keep folding the meringue and matcha mixture until it's really smooth, evenly colored, and when you lift the spatula the mixture falls in a ribbon and blends back into the bowl without a trace.

7 Line 2 baking sheets with baking parchment.

8 Spoon the meringue mixture into a pastry bag fitted with a wide round tip and pipe circles of 1½ in (3.5cm) diameter onto the baking parchment using all the mixture. Set aside to rest for 30 minutes. Preheat the oven to 325°F/170°C.

9 Bake the macarons for 12–14 minutes until set. Keep checking after 12 minutes to make sure they don't brown. Carefully slide the baking parchment off the baking sheets onto a cool surface and leave to cool. Then peel off the baking parchment.

10 Meanwhile, to make the matcha buttercream filling: Whisk the butter until fluffy in a food mixer or with an electric whisk and then beat in the confectioner's sugar and matcha powder. Add the milk and whisk until thick and smooth.

11 Sandwich the buttercream between the macarons halves. You can smear it on with a teaspoon, but it looks neater and more professional if you pipe it.

12 Store the macarons in an airtight container in the fridge.

Raisin, oat, and matcha cookies

These irresistible crispy green cookies are perfect when you have friends over for a cup of matcha! No need for guilt when you take your second or third . . .

**MAKES ABOUT
30 COOKIES**

*1 cup (125g) raisins
1 cup (200g) butter
1 cup (200g) soft brown sugar
2 large eggs
1 tsp vanilla extract
1¼ cups (125g) rolled oats
2½ cups (275g) all-purpose
   flour, sifted
1½ tsp matcha powder
1 tsp baking soda
1 tsp ground cinnamon
½ tsp grated nutmeg
pinch of salt*

1 Preheat the oven to 350°F/180°C. Line 2 baking sheets with baking parchment.

2 Put the raisins in a bowl and cover with boiling water. Set aside to soak for 20–30 minutes. (They will swell and become plump.) Drain and reserve the soaking liquid.

3 In a food mixer or using an electric whisk, beat the butter and sugar until pale, light, and fluffy. Beat in the eggs, one a time, and then the vanilla.

4 Add the oats, flour, matcha powder, baking soda, cinnamon, nutmeg, salt, and raisins. Mix to a soft dough, adding some of the reserved soaking liquid or a little milk if the mixture is too dry.

5 Using a tablespoon, drop spoonfuls of the mixture onto the lined baking sheets and flatten slightly with your hand. Make sure there's plenty of space between them because they'll spread out during cooking.

6 Bake for 12–15 minutes until golden brown. Cool on the baking sheets or transfer to a wire rack. Store in an airtight container.

VARIATIONS
• For neater cookies, chill the dough in the fridge for 30 minutes before rolling it out and cutting it with a cookie cutter. Bake as above.
• Substitute dried cranberries, cherries, or blueberries for the raisins. There's no need to soak them.
• For extra texture, add 2–3 tbsp of sunflower seeds to the mix.

Desserts

Matcha soufflés

These beautifully light, vibrant green soufflés are real showstoppers. If you'd rather make one large soufflé, simply bake for a little longer—about 25–30 minutes.

MAKES 4 SOUFFLÉS

melted butter for greasing
¼ cup (60g) superfine sugar,
  plus extra for coating
½ cup (100ml) heavy cream
1 tbsp all-purpose flour
3 tsp cornstarch
1 tbsp matcha powder
½ cup (125ml) milk
2 egg yolks
4 egg whites
confectioner's sugar for dusting

1 Preheat the oven to 350°F/180°C. Brush the insides of four large ramekins with melted butter and then lightly coat with superfine sugar. Chill in the fridge while you make the soufflés.

2 Stir the cream, flour, cornstarch, and matcha powder together in a large bowl and then whisk until smooth and no clumps of matcha remain.

3 Heat the milk in a large saucepan over medium heat. As soon as it starts to boil, remove from the heat and immediately start whisking it, a little at a time, into the matcha mixture until smooth.

4 Return the mixture to the saucepan and beat continuously over a low heat until thick and smooth. Use an electric whisk to make this easier.

5 Beat the egg yolks and superfine sugar together in a bowl until thick and then beat them into the matcha mixture, taking the saucepan off the heat to do so. Return the saucepan to the heat and keep whisking until you have a thick custard. Set aside to cool.

6 Meanwhile, beat the egg whites in a dry bowl until soft peaks form. Gently fold them into the cooled matcha custard, using a spatula or large metal spoon.

7 When the mixture is evenly colored throughout, divide it between the chilled ramekins, filling them to the top. Level the surface of each soufflé and gently run a step-palette knife or your thumbnail around the edge.

8 Place the ramekins on a baking sheet and cook for 10–12 minutes until well risen and just starting to color on top. Dust lightly with confectioner's sugar and serve immediately.

VARIATION
• Instead of coating the insides of the ramekins with sugar, try grated semisweet chocolate.

Mini matcha cheesecakes

Try using your favorite biscuits to make the base—Oreos (without the filling), graham crackers, or oat biscuits all work particularly well.

MAKES 4 MINI CHEESECAKES

1 cup (250g) cream cheese or
　farmer's cheese
1 tsp vanilla extract
4 tbsp superfine sugar
1 tbsp matcha powder, plus extra
　for sprinkling
5 tbsp warm water
4 sheets leaf gelatine
1½ cups (350ml) heavy cream

FOR THE COOKIE BASE
3 tbsp butter
1 tbsp corn syrup
5 oz (150g) gingersnaps

1 To make the cookie base: Melt the butter with the corn syrup in a saucepan over low heat. Pulse the gingersnaps to crumbs in a food processor and stir into the melted butter.

2 Divide the mixture between four large ramekins or four 4 in (10cm) ring molds placed on a baking sheet lined with baking parchment. Press down firmly with the back of a spoon to level.

3 In a bowl, beat the cream cheese or farmer's cheese with the vanilla and sugar.

4 Stir the matcha powder into the warm water, whisking until well mixed with no lumps.

5 Put the gelatine sheets in a dish of cold water and leave to soak for 5 minutes until softened, then remove and squeeze out any excess water.

6 Heat ½ cup (100ml) of the cream in a small saucepan over low heat. When it's warm, remove from the heat and stir the gelatine into the cream until it dissolves.

7 Stir the cream mixture into the cream cheese mixture with the matcha until well mixed. Chill in the fridge for about 10 minutes until it begins to set.

8 Meanwhile, whip the rest of the cream in a mixing bowl until it forms soft peaks. Fold gently into the cream cheese mixture with a spatula.

9 Divide between the molds or ramekins and smooth the tops with a step-palette knife. Chill in the fridge for at least 4 hours until thoroughly set.

10 Serve in the ramekins or turn the mini cheesecakes out of the molds by gently running a knife around the edge. Decorate by sprinkling with a little matcha powder.

VARIATIONS
• Instead of vanilla extract, flavor the cheesecake with grated lime or lemon zest.
• Decorate the tops with chocolate curls or fresh fruit.

Chocolate and matcha tart

This tart is stunning when topped with plain or white chocolate shards or shavings. A simple, light dusting of confectioner's sugar also works very well, and it gets even better if you serve it with fresh raspberries or strawberries and crème fraîche.

SERVES 8–10

14 oz (400g) white chocolate,
   roughly chopped
1¼ cups (300ml) heavy cream
a few drops of vanilla extract
1 tbsp matcha powder
chocolate shavings for garnish

FOR THE CHOCOLATE PIE SHELL

1½ cups (175g) all-purpose flour,
   plus extra for dusting
½ cup (40g) cocoa powder
⅔ cup (85g) confectioner's sugar
1¼ sticks (150g) butter, cut
   into small pieces, plus extra
   for greasing
2 egg yolks

1 To make the chocolate pie shell: Sift the flour, cocoa powder, and confectioner's sugar into a large bowl. Rub in the butter with your fingertips until the mixture resembles breadcrumbs. Stir in the egg yolks until you have a soft dough. If it's too dry and crumbly, add a little cold water, 1 tbsp at a time.

2 Put the dough in a plastic bag or wrap in plastic wrap and chill in the fridge for at least 30 minutes.

3 Preheat the oven to 325°F/170°C. Roll out the dough on a lightly floured surface. Place it in a lightly greased 9 in (23cm) loose-bottomed tart pan. Line the top with a sheet of baking parchment and cover with baking beans. Place on a baking sheet.

4 Bake the tart "blind" for 20–25 minutes. Remove the baking parchment and beans and pop back into the oven for 10–15 minutes until the pastry is cooked and crisp. Set aside to cool.

5 To make the filling: Melt the white chocolate in a heatproof bowl placed over a saucepan of gently simmering water (a bain-marie), then remove from the heat.

6 Heat the cream in a small saucepan until it starts to boil. Beat into the melted chocolate with the vanilla extract and matcha powder, whisking until there are no lumps and the mixture is evenly colored.

7 Pour the chocolate mixture into the pie shell and allow to cool a little. Chill in the fridge for at least 2 hours until set before turning out the tart onto a plate and sprinkling with chocolate shavings to serve.

VARIATION
• If you prefer, make a cookie base with crushed Oreos, melted butter, and melted semisweet chocolate (page 142).

White chocolate matcha mousse

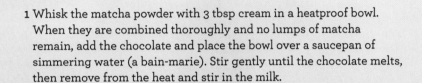

You can't go wrong with the combination of white chocolate and matcha—these two ingredients taste sublime together and work brilliantly in this pretty dessert.

SERVES 6

2 tsp matcha powder
1¼ cups (300ml) heavy cream
9 oz (250g) white chocolate,
   roughly chopped
½ cup (125ml) milk
few drops of vanilla extract
3 egg whites
shaved white chocolate
   and fresh seasonal berries
   for garnish

1 Whisk the matcha powder with 3 tbsp cream in a heatproof bowl. When they are combined thoroughly and no lumps of matcha remain, add the chocolate and place the bowl over a saucepan of simmering water (a bain-marie). Stir gently until the chocolate melts, then remove from the heat and stir in the milk.

2 In a bowl, whisk the remaining cream with the vanilla until it forms soft peaks.

3 In another dry bowl, beat the egg whites until fluffy and they form stiff peaks.

4 With a spatula or metal spoon, gently fold the melted chocolate mixture into the beaten egg whites until thoroughly mixed. Next, fold in the whipped cream, as gently and lightly as possible.

5 Divide the mixture between six ramekins and chill in the fridge for at least 2–3 hours until set.

6 Garnish with white chocolate shavings or curls and fresh raspberries, strawberries, or redcurrants.

VARIATIONS
• Instead of vanilla, try using cardamom. Remove the seeds from 6 pods and place with the milk in a small saucepan. Heat gently and then bring to a boil. Remove from the heat and leave to infuse before straining and adding to the melted chocolate as above.
• Decorate the mousses by dusting them with cocoa powder.

No-bake matcha freezer cake

Truly decadent, with a wonderful hit of matcha goodness, this tastes lovely with strawberry coulis, and it goes great with a scoop of matcha ice cream (page 150).

SERVES 6

11 oz (300g) graham crackers
½ cup (125g) butter
2½ cups (600ml) heavy cream
1 tbsp matcha powder
2¼ cups (500g) mascarpone
grated zest of 1 lemon
¾ cup (80g) superfine sugar
4 cups (450g) fresh berries (raspberries or halved strawberries)
1 cup (125g) hazelnuts, toasted and halved
semisweet chocolate curls or shards for garnish

FOR THE RASPBERRY COULIS
1½ cups (175g) raspberries
1 tbsp confectioner's sugar
juice of ½ lemon

1 Line the base of a 10 in (25cm) loose-bottomed cake pan with baking parchment.

2 To make the cookie base: Crush the cookies by placing them in a plastic bag and bashing them with a rolling pin, or pulse in a blender or food processor until they resemble breadcrumbs.

3 Melt the butter in a saucepan over low heat and then stir in the crushed cookies. Spoon into the lined pan and press down well with the back of a spoon to level the top. Chill in the fridge for 30 minutes.

4 Meanwhile, to make the raspberry coulis: Pulse the raspberries in a food processor or blender until smooth. Add the confectioner's sugar and pulse again briefly. Pass through a sieve, discard any seeds, and stir in the lemon juice. Set aside.

5 In a bowl, whip the cream and matcha powder until thick and uniformly green. Add the mascarpone, lemon zest, and sugar and fold in gently until thoroughly mixed and smooth. Fold in the berries and hazelnuts.

6 Spoon the mixture into the pan, covering the cookie base, and smooth the top. Wrap in aluminum foil and place in the freezer. Freeze for at least 5 hours.

7 When ready to serve, garnish with chocolate curls or shards. Allow the cake to stand at room temperature for about 15–20 minutes before removing from the pan and cutting into slices. Serve with raspberry coulis.

VARIATIONS
• Vary the fruit and nuts: try blueberries, redcurrants, or even peaches with almond slices or chunks.
• Use gingersnaps instead of graham crackers, or add a little ground cinnamon to the crumb and melted butter mix.

Chocolate chip and matcha ice cream

This gorgeously green ice cream is a real crowd-pleaser. To make a plain version, omit the grated chocolate—and don't forget to try it with the Chocolate and matcha tart (page 144).

SERVES 6

1 cup (250ml) milk
1 tbsp matcha powder
6 egg yolks
½ cup (150g) superfine sugar
2 cups (500ml) heavy cream
1½ oz (40g) semisweet chocolate (70% cocoa solids), roughly grated

1 Heat the milk in a saucepan. Stir 2 tbsp warm milk (not too hot, nor too cold) into the matcha powder in a small bowl. Mix well to eliminate any lumps.

2 Beat the egg yolks and sugar together in a bowl until fluffy and light. Bring the milk to a boil and then whisk into the egg mixture. Pour it back into the warm saucepan and heat gently over a low heat, stirring all the time, until the custard thickens and coats the back of the spoon. Stir in the matcha mixture and set aside to cool.

3 Whip the cream until it forms soft peaks and gently fold it into the cooled matcha custard.

4 You can freeze this in an ice cream maker, according to the manufacturer's instructions, and add the grated chocolate at the end.

5 Alternatively, pour the matcha ice cream mixture into a container, then cover and freeze for 3–4 hours until softly frozen and setting round the edges.

6 Remove from the freezer and transfer the ice cream to a food mixer or processor and mix briefly to break up any ice crystals and make it slushy. Fold in the grated chocolate and spoon back into the container. Cover and freeze for a few hours or overnight until frozen.

7 Remove from the freezer about 15–20 minutes before serving to soften the ice cream slightly.

VARIATIONS
• Try using white instead of semisweet chocolate.
• For a minty version, add a dash of peppermint extract or steep some fresh mint leaves in the warm milk to add a subtle flavor and aroma.

Coconut and matcha ice cream

Making ice cream is so satisfying. Making green matcha ice cream is even more satisfying. This tastes simply amazing, and is perfect on a hot summer's day.

SERVES 4

*1 can (14oz/400g) full-fat
    coconut milk*
1 tbsp cornstarch
1 tbsp matcha powder
½ cup (85g) superfine sugar
*2 tbsp agave syrup or
    maple syrup*
3 tbsp coconut cream
grated zest of 1 lime
toasted coconut for garnish

1 Heat the coconut milk gently in a saucepan over low heat. Put 4 tbsp of the warm milk in a small bowl and mix with the cornstarch and matcha powder until smooth and lump-free.

2 Add the sugar to the saucepan and stir over low heat until dissolved. Turn up the heat and, as soon as it starts to boil, stir in the cornstarch and matcha mixture. Reduce the heat and stir gently for 2–3 minutes until slightly thickened, creamy, and smooth.

3 Remove from the heat and stir in the agave or maple syrup, coconut cream, and lime zest. Set aside to cool.

4 Transfer to an ice cream maker and follow the manufacturer's instructions.

5 Alternatively, spoon into a container, cover with a lid and freeze for 3–4 hours until frozen slightly and setting around the edges.

6 Remove from the freezer and transfer the ice cream to a food mixer or processor and mix briefly to break up any ice crystals and make it slushy. Retun to the container, cover, and freeze for a few hours or overnight until frozen. For really smooth ice cream, repeat the process again 3–4 hours later before freezing overnight.

7 Remove the ice cream from the freezer about 15–20 minutes before serving to soften it slightly. Serve in scoops sprinkled with toasted coconut.

VARIATIONS
• Instead of lime zest, add a few drops of vanilla extract for flavoring.
• Sprinkle the ice cream with cacao nibs, fresh pomegranate seeds, or sliced almonds.

Matcha mochi ice cream balls

This is a wonderful, traditional Japanese sweet treat. Make your matcha ice cream following the recipe on page 150 (omitting the chocolate) or page 151.

MAKES 9 BALLS

9 small scoops of matcha ice cream (pages 150 or 151)
1 cup (150g) glutinous rice flour
pinch of salt
¾ cup (175ml) cold water
¼ cup (60g) superfine sugar
1 tsp matcha powder
cornstarch for dusting

1 Scoop the matcha ice cream into 9 cupcake liners. Alternatively, line 9 cups of a cardboard egg carton with plastic wrap and put a scoop into each cup. Cover the scoops with plastic wrap and freeze for 2–3 hours until they are frozen solid.

2 To make the mochi dough, mix the rice flour, salt, and water in a microwave-safe bowl. Add the sugar, stirring until smooth, and then whisk in the matcha powder. You should end up with a smooth mixture without any clumps of matcha.

3 Cover the bowl with plastic wrap and microwave on high for 1 minute. Uncover the bowl and stir. Cover and microwave for 1 more minute, and then repeat this process again. If there's still some liquid left, keep microwaving for 30 seconds at a time until the dough is thick, gelatinous, and sticky.

4 Dust a clean surface with plenty of cornstarch and place the ball of dough on top. Sprinkle with more cornstarch and press the dough out with your hands or roll out with a rolling pin to a square, about ¼ in (6mm) thick. Cut into 9 equal squares and leave to cool.

5 Remove a frozen ice cream ball from the plastic wrap and place on a cooled dough square. Quickly gather the dough around the ball to cover it completely, pinching the ends together neatly to seal it. Trim off and discard any excess dough. You need to work fast or the ice cream will melt. Cover the ball with plastic wrap and replace in the cupcake liner or egg carton and freeze immediately. Repeat this with the other 8 ice cream balls.

6 Freeze for about 2 hours until the matcha mochi are frozen and firm. Remove from the freezer a few minutes before serving.

Matcha yogurt pops

SUPER-HEALTHY

Our nutritionists believe that, as far as ice pops go, "there's plenty of good stuff packed into these refreshing treats, notably protein and calcium from the yogurt and the polyphenol-packed matcha." Just add summer sunshine for vitamin D!

MAKES 6 ICE POPS

2 cups (500g) Greek yogurt
with honey
2 tsp matcha powder
few drops of vanilla extract

1 Whisk together one-fifth of the Greek yogurt with the matcha powder until smooth, lump-free, and uniformly colored.

2 Mix the remaining yogurt with the vanilla extract in another bowl.

3 Divide the matcha yogurt mixture between 6 ice pop molds and top with the remaining vanilla yogurt mixture.

4 Insert an ice pop stick into the center of each ice pop and freeze for a few hours or overnight until well frozen.

5 To serve, hold the molds under cold running water and then ease out the frozen yogurt pops.

VARIATIONS
• For a dairy-free version, use soy yogurt.
• Try stirring some mochi pieces (page 155), fresh blueberries, or small chunks of peeled, pitted lychees into the yogurt mixture before freezing.
• Instead of separating the yogurt mixtures, mix everything together and then add a mashed ripe avocado together with 2–3 tbsp almond milk. Blend well, spoon into the molds, and freeze as above.

ACKNOWLEDGMENTS

We thank the teapigs team for making matcha "a thing." Big thanks to **Sofia, Charlotte L., Charlotte N.,** and **Anna** for working so hard on the delicious matcha recipes (and eating the delicious matcha products!). Thanks also to all our lovely trade customers, who have supported the growth of this magical green tea.

PICTURE CREDITS

The publisher thanks the following sources for their kind permission to reproduce the photographs in this book:
Page 1 teapigs; 2 Getty Images/Westend61; 4 Jacqui Small; 5 Jacqui Small; 7 (tl) iStock /kalasek; 7 (tr) iStock/RyanJLane; 7 (tc) teapigs; 7 (cla) Alamy Stock Photo/Keith Levit; 7 (cra) Alamy Stock Photo/Aflo Co., Ltd; 7 (clb) Shutterstock/BoKehMan27; 7 (cb) Shutterstock/vapadi; 7 (crb) teapigs; 7 (bl) Getty Images/Pathara Buranadilok; 7 (br) Shutterstock/Komsan Somthi; 8–9 Jacqui Small; 10 (br) Alamy Stock Photo/Uber Bilder; 11 (cl) Alamy Stock Photo / Ruby; 12 (b) Alamy Stock Photo/Glasshouse Images; 13 (tl) Getty Images/Popperfoto; 15 (c) Getty Images/ARO @ PHOTOGRAPHY; 16 (b) Alamy Stock Photo/Oote Boe Ph; 20–21 Jacqui Small; 22 (bl) Alamy Stock Photo/Japan Stock Photography; 23 Alamy Stock Photo/PhotoAlto sas; 24 (cl) 123rf/Diana Taliun; 24 (cr) 123rf/Baramee Thaweesombat; 24 (bl) teapigs; 24 (br) 123rf/sahua; 25 (cl, bl and cr) 123rf/sahua; 29 (bl) teapigs; 29 (br) Alamy Stock Photo/Japan Stock Photography; 31 (t) Alamy Stock Photo/epa european pressphoto agency b.v; 31 (bl) Getty Images/ Sankei/Contributor; 31 (br) Alamy Stock Photo/epa european pressphoto agency b.v; 32–33 teapigs; 34 Jacqui Small; 35 Alamy Stock Photo/PhotoCuisine; 37 Jacqui Small; 42–3 Jacqui Small; 45 (tl) Jacqui Small; 45 (cl) 123rf/ziashusha; 45(c) 123rf/Anna Pustynnikova; 45 (bl) Shutterstock / Anna Pustynnikova; 45 (bc) iStock/hirenman69; 45 (br) iStock/Joey333; 47 (tr) Alamy Stock Photo/Richard Watkins; 47 (cr) Shutterstock/Selinofoto; 47 (fcr) Shutterstock/Elena Demyanko; 47 (bl) 123rf/Dontree Malaimarn; 47 (br) Jacqui Small; 48 (tr) Tondaya, Kyoto; 49 (tr) Winstons Coffee, Hong Kong; all photos pages 50–157 Jacqui Small.

REFERENCES

Page 36:

1. Yusuf, Irby, Katiyar and Elmets. "Photoprotective effects of green tea polyphenols," *Photodermatol Photoimmunol Photomed* (2007): 23: 48–56.

Pages 38–9:

1. Zheng, Jusheng, et al. "Green tea and black tea consumption and prostate cancer risk: an exploratory meta-analysis of observational studies." *Nutrition and cancer* 63.5 (2011): 663–672.

2. Kang, Hyunseok, et al. "Green tea consumption and stomach cancer risk: a meta-analysis." *Epidemiology and health* 32 (2010): e2010001.

3. Tang, Naping, et al. "Green tea, black tea consumption and risk of lung cancer: a meta-analysis." *Lung cancer* 65.3 (2009): 274–283.

4. Ogunleye, Adeyemi A., Fei Xue, and Karin B. Michels. "Green tea consumption and breast cancer risk or recurrence: a meta-analysis." *Breast cancer research and treatment* 119.2 (2010): 477–484.

5. Onakpoya, I., et al. "The effect of green tea on blood pressure and lipid profile: A systematic review and meta-analysis of randomized clinical trials." *Nutrition, Metabolism and Cardiovascular Diseases* 24.8 (2014): 823–836.

6. Kuriyama, Shinichi, et al. "Green tea consumption and mortality due to cardiovascular disease, cancer, and all causes in Japan: the Ohsaki study." *Jama* 296.10 (2006): 1255–1265.

7. Liu, Kai, et al. "Effect of green tea on glucose control and insulin sensitivity: a meta-analysis of 17 randomized controlled trials." *The American journal of clinical nutrition* 98.2 (2013): 340–348.

8. Jing, Yali, et al. "Tea consumption and risk of type 2 diabetes: a meta-analysis of cohort studies." *Journal of general internal medicine* 24.5 (2009): 557–562.

9. Yang, Jian, et al. "Tea consumption and risk of type 2 diabetes mellitus: a systematic review and meta-analysis update." *BMJ open* 4.7 (2014): e005632.

10. Shen, Chwan-Li, Ming-Chien Chyu, and Jia-Sheng Wang. "Tea and bone health: steps forward in translational nutrition." *The American journal of clinical nutrition* 98.6 (2013): 1694S–1699S.

11. Wu, ChihHsing, et al. "Relationship among habitual tea consumption, percent body fat, and body fat distribution." *Obesity research* 11.9 (2003): 1088–1095.

12. Hursel, Rick, and Margriet S. Westerterp-Plantenga. "Catechin- and caffeine-rich teas for control of body weight in humans." *The American journal of clinical nutrition* 98.6 (2013): 1682S–1693S.

INDEX